Field Notes on Language and Kinship

FIELD NOTES ON LANGUAGE AND KINSHIP

by
Tyler Chadwick

artwork by
Susan Krueger-Barber

MORMON ARTISTS GROUP

Poems in this collection have previously appeared in various places, sometimes in slightly different versions: "Roadscape, with a Cricket's Chirr" (as "Landscape, with a Cricket's Chirr"), "Watching the Sunrise in St. George, Utah, May 10, 2008" (as "Watching the Sunrise in St. George, Utah"), "Litany, with Wings," "After *Winter Nursing* by J. Kirk Richards," "Self portrait with closed eyes," "For the Sycamore," and "Pater Noster" in *Irreantum*; "Wayplace" and "Siren" in *Black Rock & Sage*; "*Te Kore*," "Vestment," "Across the Hokianga," "Pacific: *Mateu, Matem*," and "Landscape, with Livestock" in *Wilderness Interface Zone*; "Mother & Child" in *Victorian Violet Poetry Journal*; "Upon hearing Elder B—— bear witness that 'Satan is real' to a Mormon congregation the second Sunday of 2011—" and "On Crucifixion by J. Kirk Richards" in *Psaltery & Lyre*; and "*Rua*: An Elegy in Holes" and "{ }" in *Likewise Folio*.

For Jess and our daughters: my breath and language and life

CONTENTS

Field Notes on Language and Kinship

INTRODUCTION

This book began as an exercise in interpretation. When I set out on the project, which was initiated and patiently ushered to publication by Glen Nelson of Mormon Artists Group and which is meant to be a counterpoint to *Fire in the Pasture: 21st Century Mormon Poets* (El Cerrito, CA: Peculiar Pages, 2011), I fully intended to pick a poem from each of *Fire*'s eighty-two contributors, to write short interpretations of those poems, then to group those readings by subject and, voila!, to so complete my first book. I wanted the finished product to be like Edward Hirsch's *Poet's Choice* (Orlando: Harcourt, 2006), a book that provides insightful readings of poems from diverse poetic traditions. My hope was that the collection of short essays on specific poems would provide kindling for readers who were interested in further discussing those poems, the poets who wrote them, and the anthology in which I brought those poets together. In the process, I also hoped to spark interest in Mormon poetry—and in poetry in general—among potential readers of the book. So I gleaned poems from those I had gathered to compile *Fire in the Pasture*, poems whose language and imagery stuck with me as I wandered again the anthology's field of texts and ran my mind over the harvest like a farmer might run his hands over a ripening crop.

Once I had assembled my list, I began to spend time with each dog-eared poem, to attend to the things that had appealed to me about them from the beginning: among other things, the striking turns of phrase, the revelatory metaphors, the strands of cultural critique, but above all, the stories. By opening myself to the stories the poems told, by keeping company with them, I began to know the poems better and to develop a kinship with them. As such, I felt more capable of approaching each on its own terms and of responsibly representing them before readers. But in the process of reading and writing about poems, something happened: as symbol converged with symbol, story with story, poem with poem, the accumulated objects of the collection began to converge with, to evoke, and to embody my own desires and memories. As a result, I became less interested in just interpreting poems and more concerned with representing the different ways living with poetry affects how I think about and interact with others and the world. For example, in February 2011 as I stood in the vet's office over the still warm body of our family dog, saying goodbye after an overdose of anesthesia had released him from the disabling influence of a brain tumor, a phrase from Neil Aitken's poem "Burials" (*Fire* 3) came to mind: "as if knowing the exact shade the dead see." As I recalled the phrase, it gave shape to my encounter with Bosley, prompting me to look into his empty eyes, to wonder what shadows remained there from our life together. Neil's phrase further gave shape—and a title—to my meditation on that encounter with loss. (Citations and sources for the works I reference throughout *Field Notes on Language and Kinship* and further information about each poets' works are gathered in Endnotes, starting on page 222.)

My experience with the language of "Burials" (as with the language of other poems) suggests how the language we read can sometimes resurface during and have an influence on the course of our real-world relationships. But in my encounter with S.P. (Shawn) Bailey's "Ripple Rock" (*Fire* 27) the order of influence was reversed. As I attended to the poem, its opening line, "This is where my mind wanders," called forth the place where *my* mind wanders most: while I'm on the road, running, my body keeping time with the earth's movements. I explore this place in a reflection on how I used to run in the early morning, which leads into an exploration of Shawn's poem (included here as "Pooling and surging and purling and cleaving and cleaving—"). So while Neil's language came to mind during an encounter with mortality, Shawn's evoked another such encounter in my mind, an encounter that has helped me give shape to the significance running has had in my life as a means to clarify the relationship between my body and my mind.

Other poets' language called to mind poems I had written during the time I was compiling *Fire in the Pasture*—poems that grew out of the intense creative energy flowing through the field of poetry I explored in my search. Take Laura Stott's poem "Across the Mojave Desert" (*Fire* 398), for instance, in which Laura writes that "the desert is full of clichés." Laura's statement, along with her poem—which rejects the clichéd personal odyssey in favor of a more nuanced representation of a person's movement through the world—recalled "Talisman: Traveler's New Zealand Companion, 1998–2000," a poem I started in 2009 when I was searching for less contrived ways of exploring what I had learned while traveling around New Zealand as a Latter-day Saint missionary. Many accounts of missionary work are didactic and sentimental and are often intended, I think, to make converts of readers—which is great if you're writing a proselytizing tract, but I wanted to see how aspects of my experience would hold up against the demands of poetry. With that in mind, I waded into the photographs, letters, and memories I have from my time as a missionary and began responding to them, pushing against and revising the platitudes that came easily as I explored my encounters with New Zealand's land and people, my religious beliefs, and my former self. "Talisman" is one result of that exploration.

While the energy that inspired "Talisman" and other poems fueled my overall desire to write, some of the language from *Fire in the Pasture*'s poets inspired original poems. For instance, Alex Caldiero's two line lyric (*Fire* 82) about standing where the maker stood to gaze upon "the splendid work" of creation—which place is where s/he unfolds "for all time"—inspired my lyric meditations on an unfolding fern frond. Six of those meditations appear in *Field Notes on Language and Kinship* under the title "Koru Sonnets," a series of interlocking poems that incorporate elements of Māori mythology and snippets of personal experience into litanies that circle around the continually unfolding moments of creation, creativity, and memory. Additionally, Lisa Bickmore's "iridescent pigeons spread their wings" from their place at the poet's feet in "Panis Angelicus" (*Fire* 52) and cast a shadow on my mind that called forth aural memories of a mourning dove's coo. (The pigeon and the mourning dove do, after all, share the same branch of a phylogenetic tree.) This coo plays backup for an elegy I wrote about my encounters with the mortality of other birds: a sparrow chick, some magpies, a crow. This elegy was a direct response to Lisa's "iridescent pigeons" phrase. However, as I returned to the poem after my initial response and subsequently mingled with other poems in *Fire*, a line from John Talbot's translation of Virgil in "An Expulsion Eclogue" (*Fire* 419–24) fit with my poem so well that I took it as a title: "there will be no end / To purling of those pigeons."

As my borrowing of John's words illustrates, many of *Fire*'s poets have given me language I've used to breathe life into my poetry and prose. I say they've given me language, yet their gift wasn't given specifically to me—it was offered to what readers may come. As one such reader, though, I've claimed this gift for myself and, in so doing, repurposed it for my own use—by which I mean that I've plucked words from a poet's tree and planted them in the soil of my own poetry. Like the seeds that pass biological material from one generation to the next, such repurposed language (I might call it allusion, but it's more than that) carries into its new context the semantic markers—the unique skeins of meaning—that evolved out of its primary frame of reference: the original poem. These meanings become entangled in and have an influence on what meaning evolves in the new context and that meaning further circles back upon and affects a reader's relationship with the words' original setting.

I've weaved repurposed language into the structure and content of *Field Notes on Language and Kinship*: in the titles and epigraphs, the essays and poems. As an example of language so sampled, I've transplanted N. Colwell Snell's "How could you not savor every drop?" from its original position as the closing line of "Vienna 1965" (*Fire* 388) to the last stanza of my poem "For the Sycamore." In the original, the question interrogates someone—perhaps the poet's younger self—who meals with a friend and a friend of the friend, sharing a sacrament of "black bread" and "thin soup": tokens of the war-bred poverty the friend's widowed friend inhabits like a disposition. Directed at the guest who has been welcomed into the widow's hospitality, the poet's question seems intended to remind the guest that the widow gave a portion of what little food she had in order to feed a stranger and that the guest ought to receive and to enjoy that piecemeal gift in the manner by which it was given: with the whole self. My use of the question seeks to draw into a new context this sacramental sense of obligation for others. In so doing, it also seeks to represent and to converse with another moment of communion: the encounter between Zaccheus and Christ beneath a sycamore fig, as related in the Gospel of Luke (19:1–6) and as reminiscent of the moment in Eden's garden when Eve couldn't *not* tell Adam that she had eaten fruit from the knowledge tree and that their story was about to change. "How could she not savor every drop?" I ask after observing how knowledge must have gnawed at Eve's lips after she had eaten the fruit and received and enjoyed the increased understanding that came of the eating—enjoyed it so much, in fact, that she couldn't keep herself from sharing her awareness with Adam, with their posterity, with the earth, with God.

I imagine Eve's encounter with the fruit unfolded gradually: from the moment she first noticed the knowledge tree and learned it was off limits to the moment she conversed with the serpent and chose to pluck fruit from the tree, hold it in hand, and weigh its desirability against what might happen if she ate. And I imagine that her understanding of the Garden and its limited space for increase grew as she moved toward the tree and considered the implications of her movement—how the decisions she made would ripple outward and influence the nature of existence. For me the image of Eve holding the fruit in hand, examining it through touch, lifting it to eat, positions her on the threshold between contemplating and partaking. She's no more the observer, passively accepting what has been placed around and before her. Instead she's creating new circumstances, new worlds, as she actively tests the Garden's boundaries and considers and responds to her environment and its potential, which includes pondering and ultimately transgressing—moving beyond—the limited language and potential available to her in the Garden.

Eve's movement from observer to partaker mirrors the nature of my encounters with *Fire in the Pasture*. As the volume's editor, I began both book projects—the anthology and *Field Notes on Language and Kinship*—from a place of critical distance where I could evaluate and interpret the poems I had collected based on their formal merit. In my efforts as an anthologist and a scholar, these tasks were meant to lend credibility to the anthology specifically and to Mormon poetry in general. But as more obligations came into my life (through my roles as husband, father, teacher, editor, scholar) and the longer I held the poems in mind and let them shape my tongue, the more my engagement of them in my spare moments and their subsequent presence in my body and my consciousness affected the way I interacted with and responded to their language, their stories, and my world. And the more I was affected by and gave way to this influence, the more it changed the shape of the story I wanted to tell in *Field Notes on Language and Kinship*. I mentioned earlier that I became less interested in just writing *about* poems and more interested in how I could best represent my diverse encounters with *Fire in the Pasture*'s poetry. As I've suggested, these encounters include everything from moments of literary analysis to moments when poems or language from poems became measures of my lived experience to moments when the language of poems called forth memories or reminded me of older poems or when it inspired new poems or was repurposed into them to moments when my engagement with the anthology and its poets just plain renewed my creative energy.

This isn't an exhaustive list of the nature of my encounters. It does however include a handful of my experiences with what poet Patricia Karamesines (*Fire* 245–46) calls "those sudden synchronizations" when "two languaged souls" realize their essential kinship as language makers: the moments when a reader and a writer converge at marks made on a page or when a listener and a speaker converge on spoken words and make meaning together. I've tried to embody the immediacy of my encounters with meaning-making by naming them field notes, a term I use to suggest that the entries collected in this book were written as I wandered *Fire in the Pasture*'s field of texts, as I encountered its language in different ways and in the midst of other activities, and as I've tried to bridge the gap between those encounters-as-lived and those encounters-as-represented. Because we experience the world through our senses, because what we perceive through the senses is limited and fragmentary, and because the processes of representation further limit and fragment what we're able to convey of our perceptions, it's not possible to fully record or represent lived experience. But it is possible to create representations of lived experience in ways that gesture toward the experience and our perception of it and to evoke in others something akin to that experience. Representation is, after all, a means of creating and experiencing the world. Hence the expansive historical archive that includes artifacts of human communication and artistic expression, all of which take up and evoke in others some aspect of the human experience.

While I try to embody the immediacy of my encounters with *Fire in the Pasture* in the form of field notes, I've tried to make my field notes more immediate and representative of those encounters by mimicking the feel of my field work: placing the fruit of my observations—the essays and poems that grew out my encounters—beside some notes that provide context about those observations and the moments of encounter out of which they grew. My hope in constructing my narrative this way—as a multi-genre encounter with *Fire in the Pasture*'s poets and poetries—has been to depict the many ways poetry affects me as a person. It has been to show how I play with poems intellectually, emotionally, physically, and spiritually—how I engage and learn from and wrestle with the world, human relationships, and my humanity through poetry.

PROLOGUE: NOTES ON HOW TO READ A POEM

Some years ago during an undergraduate literature course, a classmate confessed on the first day our reading assignment included some poems that "Interpreting poetry is not my forte." The student's confession still catches my ear. I hear her/him repeating it poetically in my mind, giving it a lyric ring that comes out more when I write the sentence as if writing a poem, splitting the line after syllable seven:

> Interpreting poetry
> is not my forte.

Besides the line break that says, "Hey, you're looking at poetry," several other characteristics give this student's language the quality of a poem, things that exist in the statement independent of the way I've represented the line on the page. The *t*'s, *p*'s, *n*'s, and *r*'s that hold the vowels in place and run the tongue from syllable to syllable. The aural interplay between *interpreting*'s first syllable and *is* as it slides into *not*, a connection that underscores the student's lack of confidence as an interpreter of poems. The statement's dynamic rhythm structure that rushes the tongue through *interpreting poetry* then slows it down to emphasize and give force to the idea that interpretation is not the student's forte. The internal rhyme of *-ing* and *-try* that calls attention to the statement's first two words before that attention gets shifted to the slant rhyme between these two long *e*'s and *forte*'s final syllable. This slant rhyme overturns the expectations we may have for the couplet's rhyme structure; it also makes the couplet sound a bit more sophisticated than a true rhyme might come across—as in, for instance, this more sing-songy rendition:

> Interpreting poetry
> is not my cup of tea.

Some people will say I'm over-thinking things here, that the confession was just a confession, no more and no less, and that the student never intended any of the above, so leave her/him alone already. And while I agree that the student likely never intended anything like what I've described, by spending time with this student's confession since s/he spoke it those years ago, by entering into and exploring its landscape, I've become acquainted with its inherent poetic qualities, which are less a matter of the student's lyric intentions and more a matter of language use itself. By which I mean that this student may have had little training in how to read or write a poem, but there are certain aspects of language—its sound and syntactic structures, for instance—that, as the saying goes, can sometimes make us poets even if we don't know it. As unintentional poetry, then, this student's statement becomes a bit ironic, as if s/he were saying, "Poetry's not my thing, but that doesn't mean I can't admit to it by speaking poetically."

My response to the confession at the time it was confessed was much less involved. As another student in the class—one who took the study of poetry seriously—I heard the statement as an out, as if this student had said, "Don't expect much from me when it comes to these poems: I don't get poetry and, honestly, don't care to learn how to get poetry." I suppose the confession could also have been intended to give the class, the professor especially, a frame of reference within which to assess the student's response to any given poem. In this light, the subtext of the confession becomes: "Don't judge me (or grade me) harshly if my interpretation is off: I'm not an experienced reader of poetry." Of course, this still allows the student to aim low in her/his interpretive performance, but it also gestures toward a willingness to at least *try* poetry, to step into some poems and poke around a bit. Ideally taking up this process would help the student develop sensitivity for the various ways there are to experience a poem and poetic language.

Because reading poetry, I've learned, isn't always about interpreting poems, even though the urge to interpret or to intellectualize is often our default response to a poem. American poet and professor Billy Collins laments how relying only on this reaction can keep readers from the pleasures of poetry, from fully inhabiting the sensual experience of a poem. Rather than engage or challenge the senses, he says in his poem "Introduction to Poetry," the only thing many readers want to do with a poem is tie it "to a chair" so they can "torture a confession out of it." Once it's secured, he says, "They begin beating it with a hose / to find out what it really means." But interrogating poems to find out what they really mean isn't any way to experience poetry. Granted, interrogation does get answers, but it gets them through violence: by provoking and manipulating the interrogated party. And being so worked over only injures and puts the interrogated on the defensive. It closes off potential pathways to understanding, kinship, and communion because, when it comes down to it, violence, provocation, and manipulation are no grounds for a fertile relationship.

Hence Patricia Karamesines' advice in "Introduction to the Mysteries (or How to Read a Poem)" (*Fire* 245–46), which rejects the sometimes violent disposition for epistemological certainty maintained by Collins' interrogator-readers: the impatience to know all there is to know about a poem, to possess its secrets by interrogating and, in the process, possessing its language. Instead, Patricia favors communing with a poem on its own terms, inhabiting its environment with an ear to its movements, its silences, its breath. She favors developing a kinship with the poem and the poet by giving way to the poem's language. In such encounters, she says, to read a poem "is not to know" or to possess the poem's secrets. "To read / is to listen from your quiet place / to the teasing laughter of some new voice" as it rises from and trails through a poem as through "a forest," stirring the sediment of desire and memory. "To read . . . is to stand with" this voice and "to move" as it moves, to let its sounding break across your soul, to let the desire aroused by the exchange shape your response to the poem, to others, to the world. But above all, to read is "never to know" the poem completely; it's "only ever to follow what calls" when your pulse synchronizes with the poem's pulse and the parallel movement evokes, among other things, desire, memories, transformation, language, kinship.

From this perspective reading a poem isn't about being a skilled interpreter, which is what the student's confession I've explored suggests. Neither is it about the attitude underlying that suggestion, which attitude Collins laments: that reading poetry means interrogating a poem until it breaks. No, it's about moving through and giving way to the poem's language. It's about listening to how the poem speaks as much as to what it says, entering its structures of syntax and sound in order to get a feel for the space it creates, to begin filling that space with personal experience, and to be filled by the way that space interacts with the body and mind. It's about seeing language not as a tool used only to leverage meaning into or out of an act of communication but as a dynamic environment our species inhabits, co-constructs, and explores as we move through, adapt to, and create our always changing world.

PLEIN AIR ROADSCAPES

PART 1: PLEIN AIR ROADSCAPES

I took up running when I was twelve, in part because my best friend, Jeremy, didn't make the junior high baseball team and in part because we thought going out for track would be something fun to do. The next year, some of the upper-classmen on the team—with whom we were or would become close friends—convinced us to start working out with the high school cross-country runners. The decision to let myself be persuaded by these more experienced runners was vital, in the root sense of the word: pertaining to life. Training with the cross-country and track teams fall, winter, spring, summer over the next five years, I learned my body in ways that helped me channel the restlessness of adolescence and that still shape my experience as I move through the world.

The entries in this section each address some aspect of movement through mortality, my own understanding of which has developed as I've run through the open air. (Hence the "plein air" in the section.)

ENTRY 1

In "To follow what calls—" I respond again to Patricia Karamesines, whose thoughts on language have been vital to the ways I think about and inhabit my relationship with words and the world. Whatever Patricia's particular narrative thrust, when I run my mind over her words, my thoughts bristle in the energy latent between her presence in and movement through mortality and mine. This energy moves me to follow her call across the landscape of words and to journey with what archetypes arise along the way to give my own narrative shape. "To Follow" arose as I read Patricia's poem "Introduction to the Mysteries (or How to Read a Poem)" (Fire 245–46), which called forth Adam and Eve's movement from the Garden and Walt Whitman's Leaves of Grass *(1855), particularly his poem "Song of the Open Road" (to which I return in "Proving Rocks").*

Field Notes on Language and Kinship

To follow what calls—

Independence Day (or thereabouts), 1855, was a watershed day for American poetry—and at the time, at least one person knew it: Walt Whitman, a Long Island journalist, publisher, teacher, and poet who some fifty days earlier had registered the title *Leaves of Grass* with the United States District Court in the Southern District of New York. Since early spring, Whitman had been printing the poetry manuscript to which his title was attached, spending each day at a Brooklyn printing shop where he set much of the book's type himself and paid for much of its printing out of pocket. This manuscript was the culmination of a half-decade or so of poetic inspiration that turned into an obsession as Whitman revised and expanded his opus across five more official editions over the next twenty-six years.

The fruit of Whitman's sowing was a widely influential American epic. Through it he introduced a new kind of poetry into the world's lyric landscape, one that sprawled across the page as it sprawled across the land, seeking to embrace, embody, and respond to the new country's varied social, cultural, economic, and geographical landscapes and rhythms. And while the verse form Whitman initiated was an innovation, because the land and the evolving landscape of American labor feature so prominently in *Leaves of Grass*, the work falls broadly within the georgic tradition.

A georgic—from the Latin *georgics*, to work the earth—is a poem of the land. In such poems, the poet works the earth into lyric rows. For instance, in *Leaves of Grass* Whitman uses language to represent and to interact with the land's rhythms, demands, products, and processes. In so doing, he shares the labor—intellectual, emotional, spiritual, and physical—required to cultivate a sustainable relationship with the earth. Such poetic cultivation seems to me a fruitful response to an environment that freely produces thorns and thistles. Hence Adam and Eve's efforts to maintain the earth and their place thereon by tilling the ground, marking it with tools; by naming its products and processes; by chronicling their movements through the wilderness. And hence Whitman's "Poem of the Road," which first appeared in the second edition of *Leaves of Grass* (1856) and was renamed "Song of the Open Road" in the fourth edition (1867).

The poem begins, "Afoot and lighthearted, I take to the open road." I suppose this impulse runs deep, this lust to set out from home, to trace the blue highways that wind across the landscape like the arteries and veins that wrap around the surface of the heart. Adam and Eve felt the pull familiar to Whitman, familiar, I think, to many of us: After they were driven by God from the Garden, the pair roamed the lone and dreary world in search of belonging. And they found it to a degree as they settled into the wilderness and learned to work the earth together, to subdue with their tilling, their sweat, their seed, their words the thistles and thorns sprung spontaneously from newly fertile soil. Working side-by-side I'm sure they learned the land's rhythms and shaped their dance with it accordingly—rising to work when the earth turned them toward the sun and retiring when it turned them away, letting plots produce or go fallow as the soil demanded, sowing when the land was warm enough to gestate seeds and reaping the harvest before the frost bit too deep.

Yet, despite finding place in the wilderness, the language of Paradise kept hold on their hearts and their tongues. Its etymologies slipped through blood, sweat, soil, and seed, bedding down in the almanac of names Adam had started in the Garden and revised and expanded with Eve in the georgics of their essential kinship with one another and with the land. Moses tells how, even though the pair had settled into the rhythms of this relationship, marking the earth, reaping crops, making words, and bearing daughters and sons who eventually followed the pattern set by their parents—setting out and settling in—Adam and Eve still took shelter in the shadow of God's voice. Sounding outward from the Garden, his song stirred the pair to worship and to movement: "Camerados," I imagine him saying in the guise of Whitman, "I give you my hand! I give you my love more precise than money, I give you myself before preaching or law; will you give me yourselves? Will you come travel with me? Shall we stick by each other as long as we live?"

ENTRY 2

"Keepers of the ancient myth——" embellishes a narrative from Jewish mythology. The title phrase is taken from Alan Rex Mitchell's dramatic monologue "Joseph's Soliloquy" (Fire 286–87), where the poem's speaker uses the language as a label for those who anciently twisted God's laws for personal gain: "the doctors, lawyers, and the Pharisees." My use of the phrase likewise twists its meaning, though my twisting is in favor of those who maintain the myths and the mysteries that hold humanity together, those keepers like the rabbis who unfolded the myth of the tzohar: the glowing stone God told Noah to put into his ark (see Genesis 6:16).

To maintain something, etymologically speaking, is to hold it in hand. This word seems a fitting channel by which to connect the tzohar's transmission hand to hand from one generation to the next with the ways we embellish and circulate stories among generations, cultures, and communities. My embellishment of the story in "Keepers of the ancient myth——" is based on the midrashim—the linked scriptural commentaries—collected in Howard Schwartz's Tree of Souls: The Mythology of Judaism (Oxford: Oxford University Press, 2004), as well as on the tzohar's appearance in Mahonri Moriancumer's story from the Book of Mormon (see Ether 2:23–3:6 and 6:2–3).

Keepers of the ancient myth—

After the Gods created Earth, they exhaled and filled it with light. This sacred, primordial glow seared the sphere to a sea of glass and fire: a Urim and Thummin through which the Gods' race—man and woman together in the garden paradise prepared for them—could watch the globe's story unfold from beginning to end. Despite having this narrative before them (or even in spite of what they saw unfold), they transgressed the Gods' commandment not to eat from the tree of knowledge of good and evil and shared a taste of the forbidden fruit. Once they crossed the threshold between innocence and the knowledge that comes of experience, the world went dark and they were escorted from the Garden. They were left with only the sun, which seemed weak in comparison to the light by which they had lived in Paradise.

But the Gods had bottled a small part of that light in a translucent stone and sent an angel to give that stone to the man and the woman as a token of their stay in the Garden. They carried it with them on their wanderings through what had become a lone and dreary world. On his deathbed, Adam passed it to Seth and Seth later passed it to Enoch, who in turn passed it to Methusaleh. At the end of his long life, which may have been extended by the stone, Methusaleh passed it to Lamech, who passed it to Noah. And God told Noah to put the stone in the ark because it would illuminate the ship as Noah and his family floundered in the flood's darkness.

Noah's story later inspired the brother of Jared, Mahonri Moriancumer, who was also faced with leading his family across many waters after the trouble at Babel had confounded human language and scattered the race. He had built barges to carry them on their way, but needed to light the vessels with something other than fire. So after consulting God about his dilemma, he turned to the records he had been given that contained the history of God's people. Noah's stone illumined his mind from the narrative and he took that clarity, climbed a mountain, and melted sixteen small stones out of a rock. He returned to God with these stones and asked him to touch them with his finger, to reach through the veil between Earth and heaven and infuse them with light. So God did. And Mahonri Moriancumer brought them down from the mountain and placed them in the vessels he had made to carry and to preserve his family across the dark sea.

ENTRY 3

The intergenerational family is the backdrop for Melissa Dalton-Bradford's poem "Bottled Fruit" (Fire 131–32) and mothers are its central figures. But the work of preserving is the poem's central concern: preserving fruit, preserving family, preserving relationships and traditions and habits of being and stories and shared memories. Hence what for me is the poem's central image: keepers of home and seed gathered in a kitchen, "cradling fruit / like a bronze planet in each palm" as they prepare that fruit to be bottled.

Apart from the way it reminds me of the traditional spiritual "He's Got the Whole World in His Hands," this image evokes Eve standing beneath the knowledge tree, running her hands and her thoughts over the fruit she has just plucked from its branches. In both narrative worlds—as in ours, I think—these fruits are, yes, just fruit: supple, sweet, desirable. But they're also much more: they're the products and contain the promise of our physical needs and passions. They're a symbol of fertility. They're touchstones, as Melissa calls them—"proving rocks," like the tzohar*—with which to test the nature of our being and the truth of our experience. And because of the stories they tell and that we tell about them, they're worth preserving. In "Proving Rocks" I take that claim seriously.*

Proving Rocks

During her prime, Grandma Chadwick was an avid hiker. She often set out along the trail network that connects Ogden, Utah's series of mountain peaks and came to know well that network and those peaks, along with other trails in the region. From many of her hikes she brought home mementos: stones from each summit that were intended, I think, to help her give shape to the experience once she had returned. She kept the collection—fourteen rocks—in a half-pint jar on her dresser.

Sometime after Grandpa died in October 2008, Grandma's body and mind began to yield to the physical and mental erosions that accompany age and she became unable to live on her own. Family members (some who lived with her for a time) and home care nurses found her many mornings curled up on the floor at various places between her bed and the bathroom down the hall because she had fallen at some point during the night and couldn't get herself up. She also began to forget as Alzheimer's settled in, small things at first—like when she last bathed—then bigger as the disease progressed—like Grandpa's name. When it became apparent that she needed extra physical care and that accommodations needed to be made to promote her failing memory, her kids decided it easiest to place her in assisted living and to sell her house.

Which meant it was their job, once they had her settled into the memory care wing of a local assisted living center, to sift through the reservoir of things she and Grandpa had accumulated during their lifetimes. A lot of their stuff became land-fill, but most of it went to family, close friends, and goodwill. When offered the opportunity to pick something from her great-grandparents' possessions that she would like to keep as a remembrance of them, my oldest daughter (she was eight at the time) chose the jar of rocks, among one or two other things. I'm sure she picked the jar because she has always been a bit of a rockhound—when she was younger, I often found several rocks in the washing machine because I had forgotten to turn out her pockets before throwing her jeans in to wash. But the collection took on new meaning for her when we told her from where the stones had come.

Rolling Grandma's rocks in my hands, I can't help but grieve their lost significance. Sure, they still evoke some meaning in those who understand their history; but the memories that give them place, that explain why and when and how and with whom each was found and brought down from the mountain, have been lost to Grandma's disease. Even the masking tape labels she stuck to a few rocks have yellowed and gone brittle with time. Their adhesive bond lost, they float between stones in the Ziploc bag that replaced the jar, which broke when my daughter took the collection to school for show-and-tell. Now I can only guess which stone was carried from "Taylor Canyon Nov [?] 1985" and which came from Mountain Meadows in 2002. At least that's where the cultural history I share with Grandma suggests the floating label "Meadow Massacre 2002" should point. The label itself seems to fit a small, angular piece of granite, but I'm reluctant to put them together, reluctant to assign the rock's origins— or for that matter any of the rocks' origins—to such a turbulent site in human history.

Geological time protests this statement, though. The earth, it argues, is the restless product of millions of years (and counting) of movement and decay; the granite stone and its site of discovery originate in and are subject to active evolutionary processes that predate either object's connection to humanity by millennia. On the earth's grand scale, then, these objects and the events that call them to our attention—the mass slaughter of around 120 emigrants at Mountain Meadows in 1857 and Grandma pocketing and labeling a rock from the same place almost a century-and-a-half later—hardly register a blip let alone make any waves. In fact, they mean next to nothing in terms of the earth's natural history. But somehow the stories we write on, about, for, and around them make each matter beyond their slight geological niche.

In "Song of the Open Road," Whitman offers language that I've used to explore at least one reason why these objects and events matter. After setting out on "the long brown path . . . leading," in the poet's present progressive tense, "wherever I choose," he settles into "the profound lesson of reception" that can be learned when we enter into an open relationship with the world. For Whitman such openness entails putting feet to earth and traveling in the open air, moving wher- ever and at such a pace as the mind and body desire. But we shouldn't, of course, just move down the road. We should also pause to "look around" at and consider what and who else the road moves and what places and spaces the road moves through and connects. We should observe how it turns no one away, how it gives itself wholly to everyone with "neither preference or denial." "The black," Whit- man says,

> the felon, the diseas'd, the illiterate person, are not
> denied;

The birth, the hasting after the physician, the beggar's tramp, the drunk-
    ard's stagger, the laughing party of mechanics,
The escaped youth, the rich person's carriage, the fop, the eloping
    couple,
The early market-man, the hearse, the moving of furniture into the
    town, the return back from the town,
They pass—I also pass—anything passes—none can be interdicted.

Because of the earth's unconditional openness wherein no one is prohibited from traveling its roads, in Whitman's words, "the earth . . . is sufficient." It provides an adequate—no, more than adequate lesson in reception, particularly in whom we ought to receive and how we ought to receive them. As the poet has it, the earth in its hospitality says, "All are accepted. All are dear to me." And if dear, we should not just openly receive them but also give ourselves to them—like "the air," Whitman says, "that serves me with breath to speak." Like the "objects that call from diffusion my meanings, and give them shape."

To speak, to make meaning: these interrelated processes are rooted in our relationship with the earth and the objects that come from our environment. For instance, I'm able to breathe and to speak because plant life produces oxygen, which I cycle into carbon dioxide and return to the plants when I exhale. And of course I have to exhale to speak: to stream air from my lungs past the glottis, the larynx, the tongue, the lips in order to articulate sounds. However, plants don't serve me solely by producing oxygen nor do I serve plants just by producing CO_2. They also give me material with which to construct an understanding of abstract concepts and upon which to build shared meaning with others. In this sense, plants become the source of some of my metaphors. They're among the objects I turn to when I need to give shape to ideas—for myself and for others—that might otherwise be too diffuse. Consider, for example, the metaphor with which I opened this paragraph: that human speech and meaning making are *rooted* in our relationship with the earth. In this conceptual ecology, speech and meaning are plants nurtured in the soil of our species' essential connection to place: the environments in and with which we interact on a daily basis. Whether or not we're conscious of being bound to these environments, they nevertheless give to and influence us and we give to and influence them. And this mutual means of influence is the root system by which we are nourished and held in place and by which we alter the soil's composition and hold the soil in place.

Whitman acknowledges this reciprocity in "Song of the Open Road." When we interact with material objects—say, by walking the earth or rolling some stones in our hands or turning to the biological processes of plants to find language we can use to better explore and understand the reciprocal relationship humans have with the earth—Whitman argues that we impart something of ourselves into those things and they impart something of themselves into us. We shape them and they shape us and, in so doing, our individual functions in the world become intertwined. I say "*become* intertwined" but that's not quite right: we come into the world already bound together. Man and woman, animal and plant: we were all formed from the dust of the earth. Our basic components— the nucleotides that make up our DNA—are the same and our biological functions are inseparable. In its most reductive sense, plant life sustains animal life sustains plant life. We're not only made of and decay into the same stuff and we don't just exchange certain biological functions, but together, with the other objects we encounter along the way, we make and remake our worlds. We co-construct our environments. And in the process, we make meaning together.

Which brings me back to Grandma's rocks and the way she named them. Of the fourteen she collected, she marked six—three with masking tape labels, three with permanent marker directly on the rock face—all in what seems to have been her attempt to position each stone in time and space, to connect them with places and events she felt were worth remembering: "Rock from Waterfall Canyon [no date]." "Taylor Canyon Nov [?] 1985." "Malan's Peak 5-9-86." "Ben Lomond Peak Trail 9-25-86." "Louis [sic] Peak 91." "Meadow Massacre 2002." I imagine, then, that for Grandma these objects taken from her time on the open road and marked with language were intended to embody meanings and to call forth memories from her experience moving through and communing with the world. And I'm certain they did just that; otherwise I don't know why she would have preserved them for so long on her dresser. But the meanings and the memories she once constructed with the rocks are gone. Sure, she left clues that I might be misreading, yet all I can do is work with and improvise from what language she left behind. All I can do is use the stones and their connection to Grandma to call forth my own meanings, to narrate and to maintain the stones with stories of my own.

One Sunday night in November 2011, the same night my daughter attached herself to Grandma's rocks, Dad and I took her to visit Grandma in the assisted living center where Grandma had been placed to receive "memory care" as her

Alzheimer's progressed. As we passed the commons area, we saw a sprawling LDS family putting on a variety show. To bring some needed change to Grandma's daily routine, we wheeled her to the show and listened together as I forget how many kids—from toddler to teenagers—played the piano and the violin and the guitar and sang several ballads to the residents and several visitors. Besides remembering that my daughter was getting antsy and kept asking when the program would be over, one of the things that has stuck with me about the family's collective performance was the father's cello solo. When his time came to perform, he sat on one of the room's high-backed wooden chairs, his cello between his legs, and announced that he would play the Prelude to Bach's Cello Suite No. 1.

The oscillations of the cellist's bow against the strings of his cello and the melody's resonance through the instrument and outward through the room were answered in my body. Once or twice during the performance, I closed my eyes and let the music fill the cathedral of my flesh, let the rise and fall of the staff rub my emotions thin. During this movement, it struck me how melancholy an instrument the cello is—how its heavy tones stirred me to longing, to introspection, to prayer. How the performance excavated my mood and back-filled it with some nostalgia, some compassion, some grief. How even the instrument's design—the scroll, the bridge, the f-holes, the resonant curve of the body—turned me inward, toward memories of Grandma, who sat beside me, age and inactivity hanging heavy on her soul.

One memory evoked by that night's recital was also called forth by the red and white marble stone in Grandma's collection labeled in blue permanent marker "Louis [sic] Peak 91." Sometime during my early- to mid-teens—probably in the mid-1990s—Grandma led me, my sisters, my brother, and several of our cousins on a hike to Lewis Peak. We set out in the cool of one July morning from the Pineview Trailhead on the west end of Pineview Reservoir and followed the Southern Skyline Trail into the Wasatch-Cache National Forest for three, maybe four miles, until the earth had placed us more directly in line with the sun. Hungry and wanting rest, we stopped to lunch—probably on sandwiches and granola bars, or more likely on granola bars and jerky—in what little shade was offered on the trail by gambel oak. Because she was always anxious—impatient, even—to press forward on the next leg of any project, I'm sure once we finished our lunch Grandma spurred us back to our feet and onward toward the ridgeline where, at mile seven, the trail to Lewis Peak splits from Skyline and carries on for roughly two more miles.

What I'm not sure of, though, is why some of us decided to turn back when we were so close to the peak, or for that matter if we were even that close to the peak when we turned back. It was likely a waning water supply, overworked bodies, or the need to get home for a youth activity that prompted the split—I vaguely recall showing up at a park later that evening tired and in sweats to play in what I think was a softball game organized by the youth of our local Mormon congregation. Pockmarked memory notwithstanding, I do remember turning back with Taryn, my oldest sister, Tim, my brother, and Andy, the cousin who's nearest my age (he's just two days older than I am); Grandma and two or three others, including my other sister, Tiffany, continued to the peak. I also remember needing to ration what water we had left among the four of us because our bottles were nearly empty, we were already edging toward dehydration because of the afternoon heat, and the hike back to the trailhead seemed so much longer than the hike to the ridgeline.

We spurred ourselves homeward by swapping leaders, as do migrating geese; by hoping the occasional microburst that misted our clothes and the trail, keeping down the dust, would cool the air instead of just increasing the humidity; and by singing songs. While my memory of much of that hike may be fairly unreliable, my strongest recollection is that we sang songs on the return journey. As young Mormons our repertoire included the hymns we sang each Sunday and the songs we learned in Primary, the Church's organization for children under twelve. These sets included songs that celebrate the Church's pioneer heritage, among them William Clayton's anthem, "Come, Come Ye Saints," and Elizabeth Fetzer Bates' Primary song, "Pioneer Children Sang as They Walked." Because I imagine we felt a bit like pioneers trekking through the wilderness, these songs echo through the canyons of my memory when I think of that hike, just as I'm certain they echoed through the valleys and meadows we traversed that day on our way down the mountain: "Come, come ye saints," we may have sung,

> no toil nor labor fear;
> But with joy wend your way.
> Though hard to you the journey may appear,
> Grace shall be as your day.

During our small moment of privation, Clayton's words may have called forth the pattern of pilgrimage that moved our ancestors west in hopes that

God's grace would accompany and provide for them along the way and in faith that he really had prepared a place where they could rebuild their religious community. And Bates' "Pioneer Children" would have offered us the grace of good humor, especially as we extended in our performance the song's already drawn out expression of the pioneer experience: "Pioneer children sang as they walked and walked and walked and walked and walked and walked and walked and walked and walked. . ." (The original line includes only four repetitions of "and walked.") While we may have drawn some measure of confidence and inspiration, even entertainment, from the pioneer narratives we mutually performed, it's more likely that any grace we experienced while singing the hymns came through the process of singing itself: through the mutual keeping of time that would have given our bodies a rhythm to walk to—that would have made us move—and through the scaffolding of language and tones on which we could hang our thoughts in order to keep them—and us—from collapsing in the heat.

It may seem a bit dramatic to think that we needed grace like the pioneer's needed grace in order to help us survive our short jaunt through the wilderness. I'm also certain we didn't consciously seek such grace along the way, say, by asking for it in prayer—at least I didn't, anyway. But that, I think, is the beauty of grace: it's not something we have to ask for. Rather, it's always already being offered in the givenness of life itself: in the relationships through which we give and receive what theologian Adam Miller calls "the very stuff of life": "Breath, rest, words, food, excrement, handiwork, sensations, ideas, bodies, . . . intentions." These are among the materials we exchange with each other and with the earth every moment of our lives. These are among the things that name our inherent interdependence, again with each other and the earth. As Miller suggests, "to be alive, to give and receive, is to be in an open relation of interdependence with the world for food, air, words, materials, sensations, and companionship." It's to realize, as Whitman did, that everything we give and everything we receive arises from our inescapable co-presence with the world and with others in that world. Our relationships, then, are a matter of grace—are *the* matter of grace. Or rather, they're the medium in which our being is rooted, the soil through which grace comes into our lives and sustains and transforms us and through which we sustain and transform others. Without them we would be incomplete because we would have no medium of support. And without that support and the grace it conveys, we would eventually wither away.

The more I think about that hike with my family and how we sang ourselves back to the trailhead, the more convinced I become that the language we made together was an expression of grace. It seemed to settle us into being there with and relying upon each other for breath and desire and resolve. This interdependence hits close to home when I remember a note Taryn left on my headboard shelf a day or two after we had finished the hike. It said something like this: "Thanks for staying with me the other day. I couldn't have made it without you." Her words—like Grandma's rocks—evoke the grace and potential of being- and making-together, of giving and receiving presence by moving and speaking and singing and resting and breathing and being silent and remembering with another being. And my present participles written in response to her words speak to the progressive nature of such togetherness: that when we're mutually present during any given event or series of events, when we're making the stuff of life together, we're doing more than just hanging out. We're doing more than the same things at the same time. We're becoming a mutual performance of givenness. And in the process we're making the space around us more hospitable, even if we're not fully aware of what we're doing.

I'm certain Taryn doesn't know how her language stuck with me, how the leaf of notebook paper she gave me nourished—and still nourishes, although it's long gone—the soil of our relationship. I'm also certain the cello player whose music still breaks across the coasts of my flesh will never know his influence abides beyond the recital he gave one Sunday night in an assisted living center in Ogden, Utah. And I'm sure Grandma never intended her rocks to become an inheritance, although it is possible that she wanted to pass their meaning to another generation, which may be why she took us on the hike to Lewis Peak that day. Maybe she sensed, as Whitman and many other poets have sensed, that "the secret of the making of the best persons" is for them "to grow in the open air," to give way to the pull of the earth against their bodies, and, in so doing, to get a feel for its beauty, grace, and openness—even of what beauty and grace Earth's openness entails—as they move across its surface. Or maybe she just wanted to share things she loved—nature and movement—with people she loved and in the sharing to spark in all of us (herself included) desires, connections, and kinship that might sustain us beyond what limits we can reach with our individual efforts to make and share symbols, meaning, and memory.

ENTRY 4

As I mentioned in the Introduction, the opening line from S.P. (Shawn) Bailey's poem "Ripple Rock" (Fire 27)—"This is where my mind wanders"—became a catalyst for my writing about the significance running has had in my life. With that significance in mind, I turned my consideration back toward Shawn's poem and used my experience to explore the narrative space his language makes.

While I was looking to title the meditation that "Ripple Rock" inspired, I reread Philip White's poem "The River" (Fire 466–67). In the poem, Philip traces the flow of rivers both real and fabled, giving words (among other things) to the way water shapes earth and life on Earth, to the way it mirrors the movements of memory. His final three lines seemed to represent well my own movements through the world as a runner, so I borrowed some of them to name my meditation: "Even in my sleep / I hear it, the river pooling and surging / and purling and cleaving and cleaving."

Field Notes on Language and Kinship

Pooling and surging and purling and cleaving and cleaving—

I can tell when I've been at my desk too long: my mind begins aching for a run. It reaches into its pocket and starts palming the stone it keeps as a reminder of how clarifying the rhythms of flesh-hum can be. It palms and palms until I become conscious of its pleas, slip on my Mizunos, and set out to wander across the landscape.

I used to run in the early morning, before the earth had turned the Wasatch Range toward the sun, before the fluorescent palette and clamor of everyday living could overwhelm my body's striving to connect through the senses with its environment. Setting out through the streets and foothills near the western mouth of Ogden Canyon, immersed in the darkness that softens the world to blue just before dawn, I let my mind slip into the silence of flesh-hum: the life-sustaining mechanisms of breath and sense, muscle, blood, and bone, whose constant rhythms and reachings-out often get swallowed up in what poet Gideon Burton calls "the numbing noise of business" in a modern society.

Such delicious slippage, Thoreau might have said of these moments, "when the whole body is one sense, and imbibes delight through every pore." His sensory immersion often came during evening walks along Walden Pond's generous shore, his self-imposed exile from the commotion of his Concord, Massachusetts community. Mine often come when I'm slipping through streets and trails on a run, settling into a pace somewhere between comfort and discontent, pressing my mind against the stress running places on the organs, the muscles, tendons, ligaments, bones, forcing myself forward. When I'm pouring my body and its sensory fire over the folds of the mind like the sweat that rivers across my skin.

Having given my mind to the simmer and slow burn of flesh and my body more fully to the senses' witness, this is what I bring home with me: fatigue, yes, and the smell of movement, wind, and sweat, for sure; but also a mind-body connection clarified like a white-stone washed smooth in a river's ebb and flow. Whereas I used to run to compete—admittedly, the competitive element of running still compels me to a degree—I've started to run to maintain or to regain this clarity, to let my body wander through my mind as I wander across land.

Shawn Bailey keeps a "deep red" rock on his desk for, it seems to me, a similar reason: as a talisman to, in his words, "pull me back"—back into connection with the earth, with the body, into memories of being consumed by the land one step at a time. His poem "Ripple Rock" begins,

> This is where my mind wanders,
> Behind this desk, bathed in soft
> Monitor light. This is where
> I levitate, oscillate, and glide
> On five plastic wheels, a pneumatic column,
> Lumbar support and everything.

Consumed by the artificiality of his environment, the speaker's mind wanders through the office, searching the "symbols" he has "pile[d] up" around him for an emancipatory sign: an object that might call forth relationships deeper than those he keeps with his commodities. In "Ripple Rock" this wandering takes the form of a litany. "This is where," Shawn says six times in the poem's first twenty-two lines, thinking on something different with each telling. After each of the first three repetitions, he considers, respectively, his computer monitor, his high-tech office chair, a "bottle" filled with "yesterday's lukewarm / Water." With the third object, however, his mind begins to reach outward, feeling toward the human meaning of what he did with the bottle: pouring its elemental contents onto his "mother-in-law's tongue" in an almost sacramental act. I say *almost* because, although his mind reaches toward the human meaning of the act, his focus remains largely on the bottle.

After the next repetition of "this is where," he moves to his computer keyboard with which he "pile[s] up symbols" like traffic jammed behind a distracted driver. Because he's just that: distracted by another, more compelling, more (at the moment) liberating symbol—"The crust of the earth." Settling into his consideration of this object, his mind reboots and refocuses, as illustrated by the next "this is where" statement, which echoes the poem's opening line and is followed by a litany of observations about the earth's crust:

> How it is thin,
> Not a walnut shell or even a cantaloupe rind
> But an apple peel,
> Three to five miles thick under
> Oceans, continents, . . .
> Thin and pregnant and implacable,
> Always sending up new mountains,

Earthquakes and volcanoes,
Always pulling high places down.

He continues, "*This* is where I concentrate"—which I take to mean that the object before him calls forth associations and memories that cut through the urgencies of business-as-usual and pull back into focus the poet's life and his relationship with his body and with the earth *through* his body. And it does this through the "deep red" "ripple rock," the fragment of Earth that represents Earth and over which the poet runs his hands. Fingering it like he does his keyboard—his symbol-making apparatus—he reads it like he might "a cheap paperback" that narrates the rock's creation "on the floor of an ancient sea" through its recreation once the poet "picked [it] up" and added it to his symbol collection.

Yet, this symbol is anything but cheap. Rather, it's pregnant with associations, with personal and geologic history and meaning—things for which Shawn's mind reaches as for a talisman when the demands of modern life threaten to drown out the rhythms and reachings out of the flesh.

ENTRY 5

The paintings of Utah artist J. Kirk Richards have been touchstones for me since I first encountered his work. His aesthetic—which I describe as abstract-realism—and his vision of the world and particularly of God have stirred me to awe and desire. Awe in that as I've held Kirk's images in mind, running my thoughts along paint ridges and valleys, I've slipped into a deeper sense of and wonder over my own embodiment and my essential kinship with the earth and its Makers. And desire in that, since I first encountered Kirk's paintings, I've wanted to respond to the awe they evoked in me—so I began to converse with them via poetry. "Roadscape, with a Cricket's Chirr" is one part of that conversation. It was inspired by a series of roadscapes Kirk painted in 2010 and is one of the poems I wrote while I was collecting poetry for Fire in the Pasture, *one of the fruits that sprang from the creative energy that flowed through my gathering. The epigraph comes from Joe Plicka's poem "True Love" (*Fire *358–59), which, like "Roadscape," explores movement across landscapes both real and imagined.*

Roadscape, with a Cricket's Chirr

. . . the scrubland rolls away like an ocean swell . . .
—Joe Plicka

Beneath the ramble and catch
of tumbleweed: the lull of horizon
delicious with distance and elegy,

dead-ends and blue highways hoarse
with the whisper of wind, dust,
wood, bone, memory—the grist

of solitude stirred up
the morning you woke determined
to pluck the sun from God's thigh

as he passed, full-stride,
over this side of town. *That's
how Jacob got new-named*, you say

when the story comes up with friends—
and strangers, for that matter.
Like when you were painting

plein air roadscapes outside Redmond
and you used it to ply conversation
with the breeze as she watched you

seduce landscape from ripples of soul
stirred by her sigh. *Yes*, you say,
that's how Jacob got new-named.

Nevermind it was *his* hip flicked
out of joint when the angel
stopped wrestling fair, wrested God

Tyler Chadwick   35

from Israel's shank. Nevermind
your layover in Peniel via *Genesis*
left sand in the visions you put on

and off like shoes at Mnemosyne's
fire ring. Nevermind that won't earn you
a cross-reference from "Jacob (see

Israel)" in God's *Almanac*
of New Names: From Michael (see
Adam) to the Present. Nevermind

God hasn't appended his reputation
to your presence on these roads
supple as a cricket's chirr

from the cleft between landscape
and soul, soul and skin, skin
and the palette you've mapped

like the zephyr's tattoo: blue-veined
compass rose sown in the right
inner-thigh, points unfurling like

worlds from God's tongue
the moment his syllables slipped
into desire, he seduced the first coo

from the fecund dove,
and the wilderness raptured
with verbs.

CHASING THE LONG WHITE CLOUD

PART 2: CHASING THE LONG WHITE CLOUD

From December 1998 to December 2000, I served as an LDS missionary in New Zealand. While I was there, I visited cities and towns between Taupo in the middle of the North Island and Kaitaia in the Northland and met people from many countries and cultural backgrounds. As happens with many missionaries and other travelers, I was transformed in the process.

Of all the cultures I encountered in New Zealand, Māori (MAH-oh-ree; the Māori r is rolled) culture has most influenced me. I've held it in mind since I returned home and many of its ideas have become part of my worldview and my writing, my poetry especially. Some years ago, for example, I began using an image from Māori mythology to give shape to a growing fascination with people and their interactions, societies, cultures, kinships, and texts. The image: someone chasing a long white cloud. It comes from the Māori name for New Zealand, Aotearoa (AH-oh-TAY-uh-ROW-uh), which means "the land of the long white cloud." Legend has it that when Kupe (COO-pay), Māori voyager and New Zealand's fabled founder, approached the islands later named New Zealand, he knew land lay ahead because a long bank of cumulus hovered in the distance.

Just as chasing that cloudbank brought Kupe a land for his people, that people and their land opened my eyes to the diverse possibilities of the human sea. I've been searching for those possibilities ever since. Every time I think I've come close to approaching some solid ground of human understanding, though, the cloudbank dissipates, then reappears over a different, distant island, compelling me to explore onward. Chasing the long white cloud, then, has become my metaphor for this persistent attempt to understand—or at least to try to understand—cultures, peoples, and paradoxes beyond my personal horizon. The entries in this section represent ways I've pursued that understanding via an engagement with my experiences in New Zealand.

ENTRY 6

Rituals are central components of human social life. As Tom F. Driver notes in his book, Liberating Rites: Understanding the Transformative Power of Ritual, *they "belong to us, and we to them, as surely as do our language and culture." By which he seems to mean that the rituals humans make and perform help us construct identities and communities. As we perform them, they take us away for a time from everyday concerns and obligations. They transition us from one state of being to another. They help us connect deeply with ourselves, with each other, with the universe, with the divine. They also create space in the social order where individuals and groups can receive sanction and support from their communities and, in certain cases, from their God for the state of being initiated by ritual performance.*

The Māori, for instance, initiate people into their cultural space by performing rituals of encounter. Called pōwhiri *(PO-fee-ree), these rituals are essentially formalized confrontations during which a host warrior challenges visitors' intentions for wanting to enter the community. If the visitors' response to this challenge is accepted by the hosts, the hosts chant, sing, and make speeches meant to weave a rope of language around visitors; with this rope, the hosts pull their visitors into the community's hospitality.*

During pōwhiri, many orators begin their speeches with the call "Tihei mauriora [tee-HAY MOW-ri-OH-ruh]!" This literally translates as "I sneeze, there is life" and refers to the first breath taken by the first woman. As such, it signifies (among other things) the principle of life that animates and sustains humanity. By beginning orations with this call, orators claim the right and the ability to make words for and in behalf of their community.

I draw from and seek to build upon these and other ritual practices in "Talisman: Traveler's New Zealand Companion, 1998–2000," which is one in a series of poems I've written in my attempts to represent things I learned while traveling among the Māori. The epigraph is from Laura Stott's poem "Across the Mojave Desert" (Fire 398–99), which at once takes up and makes less commonplace the clichés we often use to describe our movements through the world. I take on a similar project in "Talisman."

Field Notes on Language and Kinship

Talisman: Traveler's New Zealand Companion, 1998-2000

The desert is full of clichés . . .
—Laura Stott

1. *Tihei Mauriora*

Meet me in the courtyard of memory.
Slide into the circling pōwhiri. Past
the Jungian Sage who's so full of His

Capitals the unconscious breaks wind
whenever He announces Himself. Past
the voyage clichés, sterile stillborns

blue as the hackney come stock
with a lover's eyes, the cold,
sea, sky, sadness, and Grandma's

immaculate hair. Past *prayer*,
half-assed hash mark
some count as a truck stop

on the long haul to God, a hasty bead
to handle in a rosary of platitudes.

2. Field Trip

I bet Moses never slipped into Israel's
circle of idolatry. Think Aaron's attempted
coup. Think whining from the caravan's

backseat: "Hoar-headed, party-pooping,
itinerary of stone. Who made you God?
[Aside, to friends:] We should've stayed

Tyler Chadwick   41

on the Nile." Well. Go tantrum yourselves
into ecstasy in that liquid canyon there.
Gnash. Weep. Wail on those walls

so ephemeral even God can't suppress them
for long. Just be quick—Pharoah's pissed
he didn't get your permission slips, the sun's

mounting sand, and the only way to quench
my parched feet is by chasing the cloud God rides
so the firmament can moisturize his skin.

3. Marah

Let's slip out of nomenclature. Let's share
you and *I* like manna the hour just before
dawn. Let's christen them like the kauri tree

we tipped into the neighbor's spring,
whittled into visions of koru and wave,
then speared at God's bosom until his

necklaced Talisman broke loose
and swelled the terrestrial tide to a boil,
steam lifting the hem of heaven enough

to show some leg. Come join me in God's
Jacuzzi. Slide beneath the pockmarked wave.
Clarify your past to a white stone

palmed smooth by the smoldering lust of the sea.

ENTRY 7

In *Māori mythology,* Te Kore *(tay KOH-ray) is the nothingness, the void, the realm of potential being out of which Sky Father, called* Ranginui *(RAH-ngee-NOO-ee; ng pronounced as in "song"), and Earth Mother, called* Papatūānuku *(PAH-pah-TOO-ah-NOO-coo), emerged. Brooding alone in the darkness, Rangi and Papa embraced and brought forth six children, each one a god who dwelt in the darkness between their parents' bodies. Because Rangi and Papa held each other so closely, the sextuplets had no room to move— until the moment Papa raised an arm and let in some light, which stirred desire enough in the kids that five of the six decided to push their parents apart. In this way—by their violent response to being consumed by darkness—the Māori gods separated Heaven and Earth and so made the world.*

In my poem "Te Kore," which I wrote while compiling Fire in the Pasture, *I juxtapose this creation myth with images of Māori hospitality and Edenic desire to explore how different cultural practices and myths have influenced my personal mythology and my embodied presence in the world. As I was rereading* Fire *while preparing the manuscript for this book, a phrase from Michael R. Collings' poem "At Midnight" (*Fire *114) called to mind and resonated with the process I tried to represent in "Te Kore." "At Midnight" focuses on a woman whose physical desires appear to be muted by the demands of consumer culture, by the "nothingness enfleshed" in her surroundings. This was the phrase that resonated with my representation: nothingness enfleshed. It seemed to capture both the emptiness of consumerism—of being consumed by / with things, a process that ultimately deadens the desire to create—and the emptiness of potential being: a void that swells with creative possibility. Both potentialities, I think, are present in both poems: nothingness as destructive force and nothingness as creative potential.*

Māori words in "Te Kore" and their pronunciation and meaning:

Haere Mai (pronounced "HI-ray MY"): (interjection) "Come here!" or "Welcome!"; a greeting.

E noho (pronounced "AY no-HO"): (v.) sit, stay, remain, settle, dwell, live, inhabit, reside.

Ora (pronounced "OH-ruh"): (stative) be alive, well, safe, cured, recovered, healthy, fit; the principle of life.

Mate (pronounced "MAH-tay"): (stative) be dead, sick, ill, ailing, overcome, beaten, defeated, in want of, lacking, overcome, deeply in love; the principle of death.

Field Notes on Language and Kinship

Te Kore

Haere mai:
            I've anticipated your soul-deep
craw. Stewed pork bones and potatoes
to tender verging on cream. Sent the kids,
brown bodies sliding between the breeze,
to gather more puha from the fenceline.
Sonchus oleraceus: slides from the tongue
into the boil just long enough to soften
the cellulose, give the broth enough bite
to open the palate, throw windows wide
on sense. To bathe you in steam thick
as the threshold we cross between words.

E noho:
            I see hunger squirm beneath
your skin. Break bread. Dip it in butter
heavy as afterbirth. Let the excess glide
across your tongue, drop
into the well of appetite, filled with milk
fresh from the coupled Void. Sidle toward
the breast. Press between her skin and his.
Join the sextuplet gods waiting to suckle,
mouths wide against emptiness,
hunger sliding between lips chapped
from too long in the womb—

ora mate ora mate ora
                        Ply your flesh
in this orgy of mythologies. Mix spittle
with the grammar of desire
shorn from Adam's side. Slip on
this red clay like spirit slips on nakedness.
A mother her infant's mouth. Meaning,
the itch always just out of reach. Slide
from this amniotic tide into the metaphor

Tyler Chadwick   45

christened *body*. Meaning *movement*.
Meaning *legion*. Meaning *drink*
from this cup and we'll help you forget to

breathe.

ENTRY 8

I wrote a draft of "Vestment" in early 2009 after looking through one of the mission scrapbooks my sister had compiled for me. The idea for the poem, which took the form of a catalogue, was sparked by two documents in the scrapbook, both of which I received from the New Zealand Auckland Mission leadership shortly after I learned I would be headed their way: a welcome letter and a detailed list of the clothing and other accoutrements I would need during my travels.

Not much of my early draft remains in this version of the poem—maybe a phrase here and a line there. But as I revised, I compressed the language so I could focus the catalogue of directions—like a beam of light from Gustave Doré's 1866 painting Creation of Light *(referenced in the poem)—on the ways I had put on, like vestments, the mythologies and the landscapes of New Zealand. This version of the poem even shows me putting on another's language as I continue to revise my memories of that time. As I was preparing* Field Notes on Language and Kinship, *I reread David Passey's poem "The Road to Vegas" (Fire 336) and had the irresistible urge to add one of his lines to my litany: "bury me in the soil of your body." So I borrowed it, hoping to return something to David's language and desire with my own.*

Vestment

Come slip between atmospheres of memory.
Knead yourself into cumulus—your airline ticket,

your pushbike, your liahona—with fingers like
the fingers of Doré's sun. Bury me

in the soil of your body. Sift marrow until you feel
soil part, feel the fern press its head through mist

then flatten against sudden emptiness. Until you can roam sky
without tripping on God's hem, can cloak in light

without singeing every shadow to ash, without
blinding yourself as you trace the cloudfire to dusk.

Tyler Chadwick

ENTRY 9

*When in early 2009 I first read Kristen Eliason's poem "arms upon arms to an earth"
(Fire 171), I had to Google the word "wayplace" to learn what it meant. After a little dig-
ging and search-term modification, Google referred me to a Buddhist Dictionary housed
at Orientalia, an online journal that explores Eastern philosophy, religion, and culture.
The dictionary defines "wayplace" as "A place where one cultivates the Way, or one's spiritual
Path. The original Wayplace was the spot under the Bodhi tree where the Buddha became
fully enlightened." In "arms upon arms to an earth," the tree is likely a weathered, square-
limbed juniper, the wayplace red desert somewhere in Southern Utah, which is where Kris-
ten's late-boyfriend, Trent Johnson—to whom the poem is dedicated—died in a 2005
accident on Gunlock Reservoir.*

*My encounter with Kristen's poem taught me language I used soon thereafter to
write about my own wayplace, which is represented in a photograph the first missionary I
served with took of me sometime during my initial weeks in New Zealand. In the photo, I
lean against a "Give Way" sign. I didn't, of course, know the Buddhist concept of the Way
at the time the picture was taken or that I would later interpret my pose as I do in "Way-
place." I simply had my companion snap the picture because I thought New Zealand "Yield"
signs were cool. But coming at the image of me and the sign years later through the lan-
guage Kristen taught me provided me with a view of my missionary experience and my
continued spiritual quest that I hadn't before considered.*

Wayplace

at the city's limit,
straddling the hill
Elder C—— could

barely manage
without getting off
to walk. Not tourist.

Not sea-veined kiwi.
Something between.
Though standing

some years distant
from this photo, I'd
call you foreign. Alien.

Vagrant from a self
Time surreptitiously
forgot. It's not

the slacks, the tie,
the shirt sleeves. Not
the name badge, words

white on black on white,
or the bag straps heavy
as a parachute harness

on your shoulders.
Not even your unnatural
lean against the pole's

lean—legs cropped at
the knee by the photo's
edge—or the gestures

Tyler Chadwick   51

you've twisted around
each hand: right arm
square to the abdomen,

pinkie and thumb hung
loose from your fist,
left hand timid toward

sky, index finger raised,
set to punctuate
the *Give Way* sign overhead.

But how your smile of a pose
says anything but content.
How your paper-thin passions

betray the burn
of breaking in new skin.
How you eventually

carved "Body + Pushbike"
into the pole then pedaled
after cloudfire

until it seared your veins
like the opening phrase
of apocalypse.

           Field Notes on Language and Kinship

"Across the Hokianga" (HO-key-AH-nguh) and "Pacific: Mateu, Matem*" are tanka, a tra-ditional form of Japanese poetry that, in its English form, is best known by its five line 5/7/5/7/7 syllable structure. Only one of my poems adheres to this structure, but with all four I've tried to honor the spirit of the form, whose grace and restraint make it ideal for communicating deeply felt emotion. "Pacific:* Mateu, Matem*" is dedicated to a Gilbertese woman I baptized in 2000 in Hamilton, New Zealand. The subtitle is Gilbertese for "my death, your death," a phrase that points to baptism as a ritual representation of life's greatest transformation: death.*

The Hokianga sequence reflects my love for the Hokianga Harbor. During my stay in New Zealand, I lived for two months in the Northland Region in a township called Opononi. The one-bedroom flat I shared with my companion was just off State Highway 12 (which traces the Northland's west coast), less than 100 meters from Hokianga Harbor's eastern shore. Legend has it that Kupe settled the Hokianga in the 10th century A.D. and promised that when he returned to the country he would show up there first. Because of this origin story, the Hokianga is considered by the Māori one of their oldest settlements. In fact, it's a heartland for the people, as suggested by the original Māori name for the re-gion, Te Kohanga o Te Tai Tokerau *(tay KO-ha-nguh oh TAY tie TOE-kay-ROW), "The Nest of the Northern People," although it's also known as* Te Puna i Te Ao Mārama *(tay POO-nuh ee TAY AH-oh MAH-ruh-muh): "The Spring of the World of Light."*

The two months I lived in the Hokianga were, for me, a long, renewing draught from that spring. At night, when the earth had turned the township toward darkness, my companion and I would walk the shoreline, alternately talking to each other and listening to the ocean whisper against land. During those walks, I let myself settle into the silence of communion—with my companion, with the landscape, with the sea—and learned to weave strands of that silence into my self-narrative. The following tanka represent, for me, "puddles of deep, sweet silence" (to borrow poet Sarah Dunster's words [Fire 154]) where I experienced the intimacy of communion with self, others, and landscape.

Across the Hokianga
(February–March 2000)

crimson-honey sky
across the Hokianga
crimson-honey tide
but no waka to pierce
the bay's narrow hips

       *

crimson-honey sand
across the Hokianga
crimson-honey sky
but only one cumulus
to lick the bay's narrow tongue

       *

crimson-honey night
across the Hokianga
but no moon
to walk empty shores
sip crimson-honey tea

Tyler Chadwick   55

Pacific: *Mateu, Matem*
(For Beikake)

both in white sarong
I bend you through the font
watch fabric rise
on water troubled
by the currents of death

ENTRY 12

I drafted "Rua: An Elegy in Holes" (ROO-uh) in 2009 after I had spent some time in my mission journals and was buried in nostalgia. I thought of the poem when I read Jim Papworth's "Postcard" (Fire 326), especially the line "I fill the miles with memory," which I've taken as an epigraph. Both poems explore and try (ultimately unsuccessfully) to bridge the gap between present and past, experience and memory. Rua is Māori for hole, pit, burrow, den, chasm, grave, abyss, mine—all meanings I played with as I drafted and revised the poem.

Rua: An Elegy in Holes

I fill the miles with memory . . .
–Jim Papworth

My journal propped to the day you dropped around the earth, passed to a point I can only approximate anymore with a secondhand map, some tacks, and a string to slice away the pudding skin of memory:

you slip through my hunger by layers—like the summer we excavated the sandbox, sank a hole so deep we could map every sheet of clay, stand tip-toed, arms raised, voices full into soil, and still hide from the grave,

though Mom still managed to find us, combining our names in the breeze—but she had mapped our desire from the womb; she knew we would eventually start digging holes to hold the fire stroking the soul's geography,

the lust that's lured me to the window of your first Auckland flat to watch you unpack: shirts, slacks, socks, suits, shoes, the nightly routine you've worn so long it's threadbare at the knees; to ease the absence between us

with a length of pōwhiri and mid-summer breeze—the line I hang memories on after rain until they're dry enough to take notes on, to slide into my billfold beside N-Zed cash creased in thirds, ridges supple from the island's caress—

like my camera lens, softened by the hands of the Māori kids trying to climb inside, to slip into this hole we've dug and prop themselves against the walls to keep our words from collapsing, to keep the aperture wide.

ENTRIES 13 & 14

In "To turn back, back to the beginning—" (a line I borrowed from David Nielsen's poem, "My Daughter's Favorite Bedtime Story" [Fire 301]) and in "Koru Sonnets" (KOH-roo) I reflect on ways the New Zealand fern frond has become part of my personal narrative, my personal mythology. As I noted in the Introduction, the Koru Sonnets were inspired by a two line lyric from Alex Caldiero (Fire 82), which I've taken as my epigraph for the sequence.

Māori words in "Koru Sonnets" and their pronunciation and meaning:

Tāwhiri (pronounced TAH-fee-ree): Māori god of the winds, clouds, rain, hail, snow and storms. He was the one offspring of Rangi and Papa who did not want his parents to be separated.

Hineruru (pronounced HEE-nay-ROO-roo): owl woman. In Māori mythology, the owl has power to protect, warn and advise. Her appearance is taken as an omen of things to come.

Whaikōrero (pronounced fy-KOH-ray-ROW): (n.) oratory, oration, formal speech-making.

Waiata (pronounced WHY-uh-tuh): (n.) song, chant, psalm.

Tekoteko (pronounced TAY-koh-TAY-koh): (n.) carved figure on the gable of a meeting house or the figurehead of a canoe.

Field Notes on Language and Kinship

To turn back, back to the beginning—

Since I returned home from New Zealand, I've held the koru in mind. A koru, Māori for "bight" or "loop," is the tightly coiled spiral of a new fern frond. It symbolizes new life, growth, strength, and peace and is an integral image in Māori art, carving, and tattoos. Its circular shape implies perpetual movement while the inner coil suggests a return to the point of origin. Maybe it's the frond's divine proportion that holds my curiosity. Maybe it's the symbolism Māori culture attributes to the coil. Whatever the case, the koru has become for me a point of meditation. I feel something of my own mental, emotional, physical, and spiritual tugs and pulls in the way the young frond holds its leaves in the inner coil even as the plant's unfolding loosens that coil, pulling everything outward into open air, into light. This perpetual movement, the kinesis, of the coil pulls me toward my center, toward that space where the cosmos gather. Where my pulse settles into the pulse of the universe. Where the Gods—the Cosmos-Makers—dance at the infinite edge of existence waiting for the materials they've assembled to spin into being, to accept the breath of life emanating from the Makers' presence, to produce an environment hospitable enough to house the Makers' offspring.

That's what I'll say happens on my more mystical days, anyway. Most other days, though, my center consists of much more mundane spaces. Like the kitchen counter, where I worked while I had no home office. Where I listened to my young daughters in the living room playing and fighting and learning their way through a new piano piece or a book that was just beyond their vocabulary. Where they spread their homework and we worked through their questions together. Where they passed as they left the house to play in the backyard and where they returned with handfuls of rocks and dandelions, laughter and tears and muffled complaints about some sibling indiscretion or other. Where my family gathers to break bread above any given day's chaotic waters, to meal together and be renewed and sustained by our daily sacrament. Where I sit with a constant ear toward their presence—how it troubles the brooding waters of my soul.

Koru Sonnets

it occurs to me as I gaze on the splendid work that the maker too
stood in the very space I stand in unfolding for all time
—Alex Caldiero

Koru 1

Let's slip, you and I, into memory's
inner coil, into reminiscence supple
as slow passage into prayer, as
unfurling into birth— Let it spoon
into the soul— Let it lap the flesh like fire,
flaming tongues' nested ripples coaxing dawn
from heaven's pit; coaxing blood, breath, milk, myth,
appetite from the pōwhiri's subtle gyre—

Let's drift, you and I, into the pōwhiri's
lull— Let it lure us like thirst to the gods'
iris pools— Let it bend us to drink—
Let it bury the appetites, plunge them
soul-deep, release them into knowing
iridescent as the body's inner shell—

Koru 2

Come to flesh iridescent as memory's
inner shell— Come to silence like nerve endings
sharp against breath, earth, flesh, night— Come
to solitude deep as leviathan's weave,
Māui's hook in the tongue, carcass hung
crosswise currents come heavy as cumulus
stalled at sea's edge, come heavy as foresight
foreshadowed by prayer, foreshadowing miracle—
Come to sleep unsettled as death, whispers

Field Notes on Language and Kinship

loose in the waves still unsettled
by Mother's burial, anguish thick in the ash
Father wept when the gods wrapped her in memory
and slipped her beneath the veil of mist spread out
to dry while the pōwhiri circles into dawn—

Koru 3

Wake to the gods' circling pōwhiri—
Let it lure you into dawn— Let it flourish
in the flesh like a koru's flaming tongues
whispering prophecy in Tāwhiri's ear—

Let their spindrift settle like styptic
into the soul— Let it cauterize
the emptiness between us— Let it sear
the tongue's buds to clarity and prayer

and speak with the subtlety of spring— Speak
the verbs spread through soil rich with the gods'
afterbirth— Press them, like balm, to lips chapped
by the wind's etymology— Let the earth's

predicates move you to prophecy— Let them
slip you into silence, slip you into song—

Koru 4

Come slip into silence— Slip into elegy—
Slip into Hineruru's omen
circling over sleep, slurring nightmare
into prophecy into the opening phrase

of apocalypse— Slip into her revelation
as she slips into her pōwhiri, slips

into waiata thick as the feather cloak
she wears to keep her waikōrero warm—

"Come," she'll sing as you settle into her
prophecy: "Taste the gods' etymology—
Let it smother the tongue— Let it open
your palate open death's palate open

your tihei mauriora out of the silence
hung heavy on each breath as desire—"

Koru 5

Let the rest between breaths come heavy
with desire, come heavy as flesh flushed lactic
while you wrestled the sun, wound its sinews
around the tongue hung heavy from Tekoteko's mouth
high in the raftered womb— Let her whispers
sidle into your mythology— Let her
conjure the gods that gestate just beneath your
skin— Let them bone-rattle just like a memory:
The summer you quartered an injured owl,
put her up overnight in a rag-nested box,
and since wind rubbed thin sleep, stayed awake
to watch her watch you watch her
through the plexiglass lid she still questions
in your dreams, her eyes wide as exhaling suns—

Koru 6

Whiten the eyes like an iridescent dream—
Inflate the flesh like a memory—
Stiffen the sinews— Summon the blood—
Beat the breast, beat the earth like an owl
beats air, crescendos from stealth into talon

and mandible sudden and sharp as death's tongue
spurting irony from gashes deep as the instinct
she's chased since she slipped from birth's perch—

Whet your tongue on the ora mate ora of the sea—
Let it pulse— Let its murmur and forgetting
seep into your soul, into your song, into

the posture you hold like a talisman,
the prayer you put on like the grave, your body
unfolding like spindrift, unfolding like an elegy—

Tyler Chadwick

ENTRY 15

The comprehensive examination process I passed through while working toward my PhD in performance poetry and poetics included a written exam during which I had 72 hours to respond to questions my advisory committee had designed to test my disciplinary knowledge. After three high-stress days of writing, I returned my responses in three 10–14 page essays, each one focused on a different aspect of my research. I was pleased with how each essay turned out, but one was especially rewarding both personally and academically. It grew out of a question regarding the ethics of performance research in which my committee members asked me to consider the moral values with which I approach my research subject. As I planned my response, three distinct experiences came to mind: 1) one of my first encounters with Alex Caldiero (Fire 82–88), whose work I explore in my dissertation; 2) my sustained encounters with speaking and teaching in the LDS Church, including those that took place on my mission; and 3) my encounters with Māori hospitality. "Weaving Ethnography with Alex, Some Māori, and Mormonism" is a revised version of that original essay. In it I weave together personal and scholarly reflections on cultural performance and poetry in an attempt to address the influence Alex, Māori culture, poetry, and Mormonism have had on me as a poet, a scholar, and a human being.

Weaving Ethnography with Alex, Some Māori, and Mormonism

I.

At the 2012 conference of the Association for Mormon Letters, I presented some findings from my studies of Alex Caldiero's performative mode of poetry and poetics, which he calls *sonosophy*. Sonosophy is influenced by Mormon theology, rites, and cultural practices. Etymologically speaking, it unites sound (*sonus*) and wisdom (*-sophy*) and represents the wisdom to be gained by listening and responding to the sounds with which we construct our world, especially the sounds we encounter via the body, language, and religious and cultural rituals. In my presentation I attempted to construct and briefly discuss the network of cultures and performance traditions out of which Alex has developed sonosophy. This network consists both of influences he claims and arenas within which he performs to audiences. It specifically converses with the LDS temple endowment ritual, testimony-bearing practices within historical and contemporary Mormonism, and Mormon claims to peculiarity, as well as with the Catholic liturgy, Sicilian storytellers, Beat Generation poetics, and the Dada art movement.

I honed in on how this network was cued in Alex's 2010 "Poetarium" performance at the Utah Arts Festival during which he stood in a brightly-painted wooden shack behind a curtained window and accepted requests from spectators for personalized poems. I chose this performance to introduce sonosophy to the conference session's crowd simply because, rhetorically speaking, he seemed to roam during his performance among the diverse influences I've cited, drawing a little from here and a little from there as he received requests, opened his curtain, and improvised responses to the audience's varied calls for poems. The gist of my argument was this: Alex's rhetorical roaming parallels the work of an ethnographer. Ethnographers study other cultures and encounter knowledge and performance traditions that prompt them to question and to disrupt their own culture's silently-accepted assumptions in hopes of instigating positive change. Similarly, Alex gathers knowledge and performance traditions via studies of various cultures, including those in his home territory of Utah. My studies of Alex consider what language and experience Mormonism especially provides him as he organizes his knowledge into an inclusive system of thought (sonosophy) and how he uses sonosophy to critique knowledge and performance traditions through animated, often disruptive speech-acts that encourage others to think and act beyond their own assumptions.

During the question and answer period that followed my presentation, an audience member asked an interesting question. "The poet behind the curtain," he said, "calls forth for me the moment in *The Wizard of Oz* when the Wizard speaks to Dorothy from behind a curtain." Working from the assumption that this moment in the story represents the efforts of a curmudgeonly old man to trick a little girl into accepting her fate and leaving him alone, the audience member then asked, "Could there be a darker, more subversive aspect to the poetarium, more than just a performer trying to entertain a crowd?" In my answer I referenced the trickster figure, "an archetypal performer," as ethnographer Dwight Conquergood explains it, who steps into an already established world and proceeds "to breach norms, violate taboos," and "turn everything upside-down." Then, because Alex was in the crowd that morning, I asked him what he thought. Shifting a little in his seat, he turned toward the audience, then to me and said, "But the trickster figure isn't just being tricky. The Wizard tricked the travelers into finding themselves. That's what the trickster does."

After the conference session concluded, Alex approached me as I was packing my shoulder bag. He extended his arms to give me a hug and, as he pulled me into his body, he said, "Thanks, Tyler," which I took to mean that he was pleased with my presentation and, more broadly, with my efforts to understand what sonosophy is all about. I thanked him for coming to watch my presentation, then stepped back so I could introduce him to my wife, Jessica, and we talked for a few minutes about my dissertation before he left and Jess and I made our way into the hall.

II.

I begin with this personal narrative because, to me, it represents the claim to "performing as a moral act," a phrase I've taken from Conquergood's eponymous essay. For me and the performance-centered way of reading I've weaved into this autoethnographic narrative, the claim that performing is a moral act holds all the water. Because of this, I'm particularly interested in its implications for performance research, especially in terms of what it might mean for research in performance poetries and poetics. On these grounds, my main concerns in this essay are 1) how my own way of reading and experiencing poetry has been weaved from flaxen fibers grown in the fecund moral soil of cultural performance and 2) how I've taken up the challenge inherent in using that permeable flaxen vessel to gather and present to others performance poetries' different voices, world views, value systems, and beliefs.

I've deliberately constructed my first concern in the passive voice because many of the experiential fibers I've begun working into a deliberate way of reading were already in position and partly formed a pattern before I consciously took up the task as a doctoral student. In this regard, my life experiences have mentored me into an understanding of the inherent morality of performance. The greatest of these influences are cued in my opening narrative by the venue in which I presented my research on sonosophy: the Annual Conference of the Association for Mormon Letters. I was born and raised along the Wasatch Front, in the thick of what some call the Mormon Corridor: the highly-Mormon-populated patch of the western United States that radiates outward from Salt Lake City and saturates Utah, western Wyoming, and eastern Idaho. Growing up as an active participant in the Church, which maintains a lay clergy and which fills Sunday worship services with speeches made and classes taught by lay members of the congregation, I had numerous opportunities to address my local congregation—to wet my hands, as it were, in the stream of live performance. Since I was given opportunities to address fellow Mormons from the pulpit on a fairly regular basis, I learned to enjoy public speaking and was captivated by a speaker's/teacher's ability to move an audience to action with their words. Because of this I consciously sought to improve as a speaker by listening deeply to and trying to emulate those speakers and teachers whom I considered to be the most influential in my congregation.

When I turned nineteen, I decided to serve a mission for the Church and was sent to New Zealand. Traveling around the northern-half of the country's north island, I proselytized for two years, teaching people from diverse backgrounds and of diverse ethnicities the basic tenets of Mormonism. The teaching experience I gained in those homes was formative; in fact, at least three things happened because of the time I spent in religious and cultural dialogue with individuals and families whose life experiences spanned the globe. First, I decided to pursue a teaching career. This vocational decision was informed by the rhetorical and pedagogical insights that came of preparing to effectively communicate my message and my passion to others and continues to be centered on my belief that words have power to inspire others to moral action. Language acts upon the world and the more I make and study language as a poet and as a scholar, the more I sense an obligation to listen deeply and to speak responsibly to and for others.

Second, through this burgeoning sense of moral obligation for how I listen to and make language, I began to consider more deeply what Eugene England, former professor of English at Brigham Young University, called "the possibilities of dialogue." Drawing upon the words of a Book of Mormon prophet named Alma who taught that "faith is not to have a perfect knowledge of things," England comments that belief in the existence of a moral universe entails, even if we don't have perfect knowledge of that universe and its workings, "a willingness to 'experiment' in new realms, to give place in our hearts for new words and [to] not cast them out" of our minds and lives before they've had the chance to develop and potentially to change us. Such faith that others' words might evoke meanings and forge new relationships in my mind and life is, I think, a sufficient cause for me to listen to what others say, to make myself vulnerable to others' language, being, and experience. It also exhibits a reaching out to others that can serve as the basis for my efforts to reciprocate toward them with my own language, being, and experience.

In addition to these two happenings, my experience with people from New Zealand's native culture—with Māori cultural performance—was equally influential. When I say "cultural performance," I'm referring to what communications scholar Norman K. Denzin defines as "encapsulated contingent events that are embedded in the flow of everyday life." In other words, they're behaviors that arise out of and refer back to the cultural lifeways that inspired them. Performance theorist Richard Schechner calls such referential behavior "restored" or "twice-behaved" because it's just that: performance that has been performed or rehearsed before, even if under different circumstances or in the life of a different performer. More than just mere imitation, though, cultural performances "function as vital acts of transfer," to use Diana Taylor's words. Taylor, a performance scholar, explains what this means: Through reiterated behavior, performances transmit "social knowledge, memory, and a sense of identity" from and to others both within and beyond the same culture. In this way performers inherently, if unconsciously, move to persuade others of the truth of their experience. And in this way, I believe, the Māori cultural performances I experienced in New Zealand exerted their influence on my life and mind.

I could share many anecdotes to illustrate this influence, but one in particular seems apropos to my current consideration of performing as a moral act: when I had been in New Zealand for about six months, I moved to a new city in the country's Bay of Plenty region. The first night I was there, my missionary companion and I visited a family who was active in the local Mormon congregation. We parked our bikes in the front yard and walked down the driveway to meet the father, who was emptying canvas sacks onto a plywood bench near the

Field Notes on Language and Kinship

home's detached garage. As we approached, he looked up and invited us to join him. My companion introduced me and I extended my hand, which the father—Eddy, he told me—swallowed in his with a vigorous shake. He was a large man, heavyset and rotund, with a shaved head and deep brown eyes that sparked with curiosity and compassion. Once he let go my hand, he asked if we were hungry: he had just returned from diving in the Bay, he said, and had some food straight from the sea. Before we could respond, he had reached into a sack, pulled out a small sea urchin, cracked the spiny shell, and offered me the first taste. I hesitated a moment because I wasn't sure what to think of the bright orange slush—the roe—I saw inside the shell. But encouraged by his grin, I slid my finger through the roe and wiped it on my tongue.

I've since come to understand something more of the gift Eddy offered me that day—not just about the sea urchin roe, which I've learned is a traditional Māori food and for which I don't have the palate, but about the ethics of Māori hospitality, which have become entangled with my faith in the power and influence of words responsibly shared. In their discussion of gift-giving and philanthropy in Māori society, Tuwhakairiora Williams and David Robinson point out that Māori generosity is shored up by "the concepts of *aroha* (love) and *manaaki* (nurturing)." Yet, Williams and Robinson continue, for the Māori "the result does not precisely mirror western generosity, for Māori generosity also incorporates *wairua* (the spiritual dimension) and *pono* (integrity and sincerity)." Love, nurturing, integrity, sincerity, and openness to the spiritual dimension of human experience: these are a handful of the things Eddy, his fellow Māori, and my experiences as a Mormon missionary in New Zealand held out to me—that they still hold out to me. These are the things I seek to incorporate into my everyday performance as a husband, as a father, as a poet, as a teacher, as a public speaker, as a performance ethnographer.

III.

Turning these gifts in my hand, contemplating how the ethics of generosity they shape might lead me to genuine understanding of and communion with others, I think of Alex. But, no, *shape*'s not quite the right word to describe how these characteristics come together. *Weave* seems more appropriate, considering the metaphor I've taken to describe my way of reading, which also has its roots in my experience of Māori cultural performance. One of the only material gifts I brought home from New Zealand is a flax bookmark. The art of Māori flax weaving has been integral to Māori culture since their ancestors arrived in New

Tyler Chadwick   71

Zealand centuries ago. They used flax to make clothes, shelter, rugs, sleeping mats, ceremonial dress, etc. The bookmark was given to me one Sunday afternoon by a Māori woman (she and her husband were both active in the local Mormon congregation) who pulled a flax leaf from her garden and weaved it as my companion and I talked with her and her husband on their back lawn. She offered it to me during the course of our conversation and I often used it to keep my place in the scriptures I toted around the country in my shoulder bag. It's now boxed away with other artifacts of my past.

The memory of watching her weave the bookmark resurfaced years later when I reread Conquergood's essay, "Performing as a Moral Act: Ethical Dimensions of the Ethnography of Performance." In the first paragraph Conquergood cites folklorist Henry Glassie who Conquergood says "represents the contemporary ethnographer's interest" in exploring the ways "expressive art and daily life, texts, and contexts" breathe life into each other. Glassie's concern, then—a concern Conquergood and I share with him—is essentially with how humans can transform and be transformed by the expressive art we create and re-create, including our everyday performances. In his studies of this potentially transformative process, Glassie confesses that he begins by considering the "sturdy, fecund totalities created by people themselves": their "whole statements, whole songs or houses or events." Then he "weave[s] contexts" around these lifeways—these cultural texts—"to make them meaningful, to make life comprehensible." Just as when the Māori woman weaved years of practice and tradition into my bookmark, weaving contexts around texts increases the texts' narrative value. By adding to each text's provenance, this process provides researchers and informed spectators means with which they might more effectively engage, analyze, and interpret those texts. But accounting for context also does more than just expand each text's narrative reach: it takes seriously the people who created these sturdy, fecund totalities, these richly-layered witnesses of human experience; it takes humans with varied and complex life-worlds and approaches them on their own terms. In Conquergood's words, it helps the ethnographer of performance "get close to the face of humanity where life is not always pretty," where the tang of last night's dinner still lingers on the breath, where the lineaments of anxiety, age, and desire etch experience into the skin.

Which brings me back to Alex Caldiero and performance poetics: Throughout this essay, whenever I refer to Alex, I've dropped the academic convention of referring to others by the surname simply because it felt too strange. Take, for instance, this phrase, which I've changed slightly from its appearance in my introduction: "since Caldiero was in the crowd that morning." Alliterative as the phrase may be when written this way, it does two things I'm unhappy with: first, it puts Alex too far away from my experiences with trying to meet him on common ground. And I'd like to keep him close in order to, on the one hand, better understand his poetics—his word- and world-making—and, on the other hand, give him something we all crave: understanding and validation. I say this in light of my reading of the following interaction: During our conversation after my conference presentation, Alex said to my wife and me, "See, I'm not scary," after which he paused a second, then added, "am I?" His question reflects his perception of how others view him—as a subversive character to be feared—as well as his quest for understanding and validation, his desire to know that his poetry is being heard, but even moreso that it's being heard on its own terms. This pursuit is central to performance ethnography and to my personal experience of poetry.

The second thing the more distant phrasing of the clause "since Caldiero was in the crowd that morning" does is this: It holds Alex at arm's length even as the memory of our embrace and his voiced appreciation pulls me into the sensuous immediacy of his poetics. As a spectator, I want to surrender to the intimacy of this immediacy, to make what Conquergood calls an "empathic leap" into Alex's otherness. But as a researcher, I feel the need to proceed with caution. Conquergood explains why in "Performing as a Moral Act" when he sketches out "four *ethical pitfalls*, performative stances towards the other that are *morally problematic*." The italics, which I've added, make this sound like serious business. And, of course, it is, as is all research dealing directly with human subjects and their cultures and lives. Hence, I proceed with caution, keeping these ethical pitfalls in view and seeking to mediate them in my attempts at dialogue with Alex and my academic and faith communities, in order, I hope, to avoid getting snared.

The first stance Conquergood explains is "The Custodian's Rip-Off." The "sin" here, Conquergood says, "is selfishness," which is caused by a researcher's "detachment" from and lack of commitment to another's culture. This lack of connection leads a researcher to plunder the other culture for artifacts and traditions that might bring a nice return on the researcher's investment once they're sold off at home. The second stance is "The Enthusiast's Infatuation," which is more akin to "singles' bar cruising" for a quick lay than to actual engagement with the other. Those who flirt with this stance attach themselves to others only superficially, identifying with and committing to them too quickly, such that the other's distinctiveness gets glossed over in claims to sameness. In this view, the other is worth only as much as s/he reflects or gratifies the researcher's self. The problem with the third stance, "The Curator's Exhibitionism," is that the researcher is more like a tourist excited by and committed to the other's difference even though s/he refuses to identify with this difference, keeping it mute by staring from a distance. Yet, *staring* isn't quite the same thing as *observing*; the former term implies voyeuristic curiosity while the latter term suggests attending a bit more carefully to the complete experience of the other. While these first three stances are all morally problematic in their own way, the most "reprehensible" of the four pitfalls is "The Skeptic's Cop-Out." Conquergood's adjective for this stance ("reprehensible") is so adamant because any researcher who dwells in this nihilistic corner of the moral universe adamantly opposes engaging with the other on any terms, let alone her/his own. Through the lens of the skeptic's arrogance and nihilism, the other is just too different, too inaccessible, too not-worth-my-time—and thus not worth engaging at all in dialogue. So why risk it?

But that's exactly what I sense I need to do in order to genuinely understand and represent others: *risk it*. In this light, Conquergood stresses that the only way out of the "moral morass and ethical minefield of performative plunder, superficial silliness, curiosity-seeking, and nihilism" inherent in these morally problematic performance stances is through "dialogical performance." Dialogical performance, Conquergood submits, "struggles to bring together different voices, world views, value systems, and beliefs so they can have a conversation with one another." The aim in so doing, he continues, "is to bring self and other together so that they can question, debate, and challenge one another." The healthy tug-and-pull between self and other, identification and differentiation that occurs during this continuous coming together makes dialogical performance "a kind of performance that resists conclusions." It's a stance toward others that isn't afraid to look them in the eyes, to engage them in intimate conversations, or to become tangled in their lives and narratives and to respectfully weave them into our own. It entails generosity and reciprocity, sensuous immediacy and making the empathic leap into the other's otherness, without, of course, losing sight of the self. And it's about weaving together two voices or more in what Conquergood elsewhere calls "the processes of communication that constitute the 'doing' of ethnography: speaking, listening, and acting together"—co-active or coperformance processes that are inseparable from our embodied experience *with* the world and our experience as bodies *in* the world.

As a moral means of representation, dialogical performances of the sort Conquergood calls for embody what Denzin describes as "an ethical aesthetic that demands that texts be written and read in ways that morally move readers and viewers." While this aesthetic asks for performance research—for language—that stirs others to moral movement, it should also simply make them move. Speech communication scholar Elyse Lamm Pineau argues in her discussion of liberatory education and its marshalling of the body that a "poetically crafted narrative can enable a reader to *feel* into the research situation, to participate kinesthetically as well as intellectually." Kinesis, then, is key to composing successful performance ethnography, the kind that feels its way from the performer's body to the researcher's body to the research body to the reader's body—and among them all at once. And one key to performing such ethnographic kinesis—a characteristic I've grappled with in this narrative (as in this book)—is first moving to meet "people on the ground of their experience by exposing oneself to their expressive performances." By opening myself to Alex and entering his embrace, I've tried to take Conquergood at his word and to exercise what hospitality I've developed through my engagement with Mormonism's truth claims and with Mormon and Māori culture by making "proximity, not objectivity," my "epistemological point of departure and return"—my embodied way of knowing and representing sonosophy and other types of poetry.

IV.

Having, however crudely, weaved these ways of knowing into my approach to poetry, I'm ready to run that approach through the stream of performance poetics. For this essay, I'll see how it holds up against video recordings of American poet Tracie Morris' 2005 "Love in 2010" performance and Alex Caldiero's 2009 performance of a poem I call "Seeing a Body." My representations enter the experience of each poem from a different perspective: both weave contexts around each text, but my engagement of Morris' poem begins in the way my body has responded to her performance and my engagement of Alex's focuses on his impact on the performance venue itself. Both approaches seem to me valid points of departure for meeting the moral demands each performance makes on me as a researcher.

In "Love in 2010," Morris performs the erotic body in such a seductive, sensual way that after I heard it the first time I found myself unconsciously recalling the movement and incantation of her words. At first this seemed to occur at the strangest times. I noticed myself reciting the opening stanza—with Morris' cadence and tone, no less—while I was running, while I was on the waking edge of sleep, while I was sitting at my desk doing some tedious editorial task or another: "Click flicker click [pause] click flicker" boring through my mind like an earworm. As I looked closer at the performance and considered the times it sprang to mind, however, I noticed (or theorized) a connection: at each moment of recall, my conscious mind was empty enough that my physical desires and rhythms surfaced in a re-performance of Morris' poem. For instance, running always clears my head and makes my body scream. In the moments just before and at waking, the body seems to spoon into the cavity usually filled by consciousness. And the editorial work I sometimes do is tedious and repetitive enough to numb the mind; with the sieve of conscious thought out of the way, the body can feel and express itself more deeply. So it seems that Morris' voice had somehow slipped into bed with my physical desires and rhythms. And while for the most part I consider this engagement with the body healthy, even sacramental, it can also be manipulated for others' gain and to our detriment. In her comments on "Love in 2010," Morris calls this breakdown of wholesome and productive human yearnings, this exploitative repression of the body, a "dystopia of desire."

This bodily repression seems to be in line with the poem's performed content: as I see it, in her performance Morris both physically and textually enacted the female body as objectified in its transient, passive, digitized relationship with a viewer who actively clicks a hyperlink on the computer screen that leads to a highly sensuous image (whether it's pornographic, from Hollywood, or an advertisement) that then flickers on the screen, seducing the viewer into another clicked link and another flickering image, and so on. Click. Flicker. Click. Flicker. In this highly sensual and consumption-based process, the images can slip beneath the conscious mind—as I experienced with Morris' performance—where they manipulate the body's desires and rhythms, which then spur us to further consumption. By breaking down and enacting this process on stage, Morris became something of a trickster, exposing her audience to reiterated behavior that was meant to trick them into new ways of considering the body and its relationship to and place in a consumption-based society.

Alex enacted a similarly embodied performance in "Seeing a Body." Through his performance, he compelled an awareness of the body's connection to the earth and to language and sound. In fact, he compelled an awareness of the body's connection to the earth *through* the sonic dimensions of language.

Field Notes on Language and Kinship

What follows is a textual representation of his performance: Rain misted the people gathered for the event, which was organized by 350.org in conjunction with the International Day of Action for Climate Justice. After a brief introduction from the event emcee, Alex took the microphone, stepped before the crowd, and laid down on the cement. Holding a hardbound tome over his face, he put the microphone to mouth, panted for a few seconds—each breath with increasing intensity—and performed this short poem:

> Seeing a body
> from the vantage point of the soles of the feet
> immediately turns it into a corpse.
>
> It is so difficult to think
> that person alive.
>
> Even seeing the chest rising and falling
> offers no surety of their breathing.
>
> From the vantage point of the soles of the feet
> it is the earth
> that has all the work of holding and keeping.
>
> From the earth's point of view
> the feet are the whole body.

After closing the *y* in "body," he finished the performance with a series of drawn-out guttural sounds, then stood up, thanked the crowd, and replaced the microphone. Yet, even after his performance was completed and Alex had left the stage area, his presence lingered: because he laid down on somewhat dry cement just as the rain picked up, when he stood to leave, the outline of his body remained on the ground. This image serves as a serendipitous reminder of his performance, its grounding in a full-bodied performance poetics, and the intended impact and meaning of his performance.

For me, this physical marker of Alex's presence also highlights—and in the process deepens how rooted I am in—the acoustic geography mapped out by performance poetics and by poetry in general. By *acoustic geography* I mean the aural composition evoked in my mind through the process of experiencing a poet's words as performed. Because as I allow those words and their sounds and movements to wash over my imagination, they call forth my embodied experience in the world. (Alex's "Seeing a Body" performance, for instance, evoked my experiences laying on the ground, eyes closed, face to the sun or rain.) By attending to the physical experience of performed language, as gained by considering the contexts and movements of a performer's words—the intonations, the cadence, the verbal gestures, as well as the performance venue and the poet's interactions therein—the stream of language, as embodied, purposeful sounds, wells up in my soul.

And I reach inward to fill my flax bag.

PANIS ANGELICUS

PART 3: PANIS ANGELICUS

Panis angelicus: the bread of angels. The phrase comes from Saint Thomas Aquinas' hymn known as "*Sacris Solemniis* (At this Our Solemn Feast)," which is sung for morning prayer during the Catholic Church's Feast of Corpus Christi (Feast of the Body of Christ), a traditional celebration of the Eucharist. The hymn's penultimate stanza begins, "*Panis angelicus / Fit panis hominum*": "The bread of angels / Becomes the bread of man." These two lines, like the hymn's last two stanzas, point to Christ as the Living Bread sent from God's presence to nourish and sustain those who will take Christ—the Word of God—to tongue, who will accept the reality of his presence through ritual communion. And one way to do this, many Christians believe, is by receiving the emblems of his corporeal sacrifice: ritually consecrated bread and wine.

I came to the phrase "*panis angelicus*" via Lisa Bickmore's eponymous poem (*Fire* 52), which approaches various acts and places of communion and considers how these places and acts help people find "a way back to God." Lisa's particular focus is on angels and birds: winged figures that traditionally facilitate communal acts by witnessing ritual performance, protecting sacred places, and carrying messages both to and from Heaven. In this section's entries I take up the same focus, although some of my winged figures hover only in the background.

ENTRY 16

In the late spring of 2008, Jess and I took our young family to visit her grandparents in St. George, Utah. One morning during our visit, I woke early and went for a run. Moving through an unfamiliar environment in the slow bloom of dawn piqued my senses such that when I returned to the house and was stretching on the patio, the avian presence in the yard was amplified. As I watched each bird do its work, the first line and a half of what would become "Watching the Sunrise in St. George, Utah, May 10, 2008" took shape on my tongue. Some time later, as I reread Elizabeth Pinborough's "Who Will Bend and Bow like the Willow" (which is part of her longer sequence, "A Shaker Sister's Hymnal" [Fire 352–56]), her phrase "swept along by movement and voice" called to mind "Watching the Sunrise." I took the phrase as an epigraph to suggest my poem's connection with the ideas Elizabeth explores in hers: movement, communion, desire, the divine presence.

Field Notes on Language and Kinship

Watching the Sunrise in St. George, Utah, May 10, 2008

Swept along by movement and voice . . .
–Elizabeth Pinborough

I wish I had known the names
of all the birds: I'm sure it was a sparrow,

wings wound tight against the wind,
who dropped to the tip of a cypress

before re-mounting the sky; and
two more circling the birdfeeder,

vying for seed. And a robin, breast flared
even before dawn,

sifting the xeriscape for a meal,
prouding its head to swallow, then

vanishing down a nearby bluff.
And scrambling from beneath backyard sage,

what must have been a mourning dove
threw dust and air at my presence. And

as we had come into town, I'm sure it was a raven
who arced across the road, tilting its wings

against the updraft from our car
to gather sky around its violet-

blue gloss. But that brooding coo,
too long and low

for the dove, covering the crickets' trill,
charming light from its clay vessel—

did Adam, at first,
even really know that name?

Tyler Chadwick   83

ENTRY 17

As I mentioned in my introduction, "There will be no end to purling of those pigeons—" was a direct response to a line from Lisa Bickmore's "Panis Angelicus" (Fire 52) and the title is a line from John Talbot's translation of Virgil, "An Expulsion Eclogue" (Fire 419–24).

There will be no end to purling of those pigeons—

No. Not pigeons. A mourning dove, its anti-climactic cooing a constant beneath the songs of other birds. As if grief played back-up for memory. As if the chorus I sing with the breeze wasn't heavy enough with desire and elegy. As if the cries of the un-nested sparrow chick I nursed one adolescent summer, whose broken legs and wing I couldn't mend—as if those cries cut short on Grandpa's workbench, at the end of Grandpa's mallet, needed accompaniment. As if the magpies he shooed from his garden with a .22 didn't still give me cheek for standing by and wondering how Grandpa could have missed, how he had taken aim and still let them fly away. As if the crow I saw roadside one spring morning—its swollen body trimmed with grass, its head cropped with dew and cocked toward the grave, top eye muting the sky in a milky gaze, beak cracked in perpetual "caw"— wasn't portent enough to mute the rasp of leaves tripped by the wind through my wooded suburban lull.

ENTRY 18

"Litany, with Wings"responds to J. Kirk Richards' series of winged figure paintings (2008–2009) and to 17th Century poet George Herbert's poem "Easter Wings." The last line and a half of "Litany" was directly inspired by two sentences from Lance Larsen's prose poem "To the Lost One-Third" (Fire 256). Addressing the one-third part of the hosts of heaven who followed Lucifer to eternal expulsion from God's presence, Lance asks, "What should I call you—devil spawn, Satan's imps, lost ones?" Then he continues: "Or do you prefer Legion? Something elegant about that collective I, that singular we." I've tried to bring something of that elegance to my poem.

Litany, with Wings

With Thee, O, let me rise, let me combine.
        O, let me imp my wings on thine. Let me
             slip across your lesser coverts like the lift
        that slips you into sky. Let me hitch
on that lift up Jacob's ladder. Let me spoon
        with your slipstream beneath the atmosphere's
             sheets. Let me tease plumes of light from the altar
        of your skin. Let those plumes purl like incense.
Let us purl like incense. Let's sear the soul's
        tabernacle, let desire rise like leaven, let our verbs
             rise like leaven, let our flesh braze and sweeten
        on God's flaming tongue. Let's *allelu* this sacrament
of flesh. Let's savor the body's carnival. Let's masquerade
        singular as Legion. Let's legion singular as God.

ENTRY 19

Before Grandpa Chadwick died in October 2008 he was confined to a care facility. My wife and I wanted our daughters to know him at least as he was during his final years, so we visited when we could. However, because I had a hard time seeing how far he had deteriorated from the man I grew up knowing and because at the time our second daughter was only two and restless (as toddlers are), I spent a lot of time during our visits walking the center's hallways, my two-year-old leading the way. On one of these walks we met an old woman whose face and voice got stuck in my head—in fact, I can still see her and hear her Greek-American accent, especially when I reread "Siren," which is essentially just a transcription of the short, reiterative conversation we had in the hallway that day.

A phrase from Timothy Liu's poem "Genesis 29:20" (Fire 266) evoked the memory of that conversation, that passing moment of communion. I've taken Timothy's phrase as my epigraph in an attempt to bring my bit of dialogue into conversation with the moments of communion layered into his poem.

Siren

A meal is all
we ever shared—
—Timothy Liu

I only saw her once. While I was pacing the halls of an old folks' home, she spoke from the crosshall—where other patients slept or stared, heads cocked against wheelchair frames, saliva fanned across sweaters and soiled linens—her hands raised, fingers curled upon themselves, tempting those who could bear her straying eye and rotten smile to share forgotten bread: Have you ever had a Greek pastry? she said. Tell you what I'm gonna do. Next time you're here, I'm gonna have a Greek pastry for you and your wife and your little girl there. I'll order some from North Andover, from the church there. It should be here in three days. It doesn't spoil. Tell you what, she's a little doll. I think she'll like the pastry. It's not sour, it's sweet; I think she'll really like it. How old's she? *Almost two.* She's kinda small for her age, isn't she? Tell you what, I'm gonna get some Greek pastry for you and for her—I've got the pamphlet in my room, in case you don't believe me. It'll take two or three days to get it here from North Andover. I think you'll like it. They gave me my Communion there. I'm Greek, you know. How old's she? *Almost two.* Looks like she likes the bird. Don't worry. It won't bite; it's in a cage. Tell you what, I bet it's hard to leave her. Is this her first time here? Have you ever had a Greek pastry?

Tyler Chadwick   89

"After Winter Nursing *by J. Kirk Richards" and "Landscape, with Livestock" both respond to Kirk's paintings and were called to mind later as I reread* Fire in the Pasture. Winter Nursing *(2003) depicts a mother breastfeeding a child. The mother's presence circumscribes the infant, who grasps the mother with both mouth and hand. I explore the intimacy of such communion in my poem, which takes as its epigraph a phrase from Susan Elizabeth Howe's "Both the Fragrance and the Color" (*Fire *225–26), which also explores communion between mother and child.*

"Landscape, with Livestock" was inspired by Kirk's landscape painting, Pond at Thompson's Station *(2008), which I describe somewhat in the poem. My epigraph comes from Sharlee Mullins Glenn's "Somewhere" (*Fire *188–89) in which Sharlee ruminates over her mother's death, remembering and trying to represent what she sensed the moment her mother passed. Both Sharlee's poem and mine consider what happens to our being in the world when we encounter moments of loss.*

After *Winter Nursing* by J. Kirk Richards

. . . a question that hovers
over her grave . . .
—Susan Elizabeth Howe

I imagine myself newborn. Mouth
dripping with nipple and milk
warm as the rest between breaths

when the flesh goes lax against
death. Stutters between syllables
of desire. Cozies up to the grave

as to memories nursed
over the mourning dove's elegy
the winter Keats slipped beneath

my skin. Nestled into the swaddling
Mother knit around my soul
before she raised me to breasts

heavy as temptation. Latched me on
to her heritage, Eve calling *come*
eat from the kitchen as she filled

an eight by three by six basin
with desire enough to top off
the abyss. To trigger the contraction

of God's womb, Eden's walls bearing
down on my hunger. Birthing stars
like purled bodies

sweating as snow down a window
fogged by childhood wanting in.
Panting its catechism.

Tyler Chadwick   91

Asking what it means when
the mourning dove sings even though
winter's come. Even though

the dove's coo may just be a coo.
Even though I've been asking
since Keats came in from the cold

when a bird's just a bird. Snow just snow.
Flesh just flesh. Death just death. God
just breath on a memory, marking

where I buried placenta and soul
in this landscape suddenly blank
as DNA the moment of conception.

Base pairs copulating like voices
singing back-up in a dream. The one
where I'm Adam. Or is it Eve? Keats?

My mother? God? Me? Sitting opposite
winter. Watching question marks
punctuate a garden: sprouts turned

fruit-bearing trees, branches heavy
with burial urns heavy with milk
still warm as the rest between breaths.

Landscape, with Livestock
(On *Pond at Thompson's Station* by J. Kirk Richards)

. . . a sigh
        or the absence thereof . . .
–Sharlee Mullins Glenn

The sun has been misplaced.
Or, if you'd like to get more
Biblical, it's returned

to the dove's abyss—or
was that Milton? I can't be sure
as I dance so near the beginning

with words so supple they
bend into themselves until
only the landscape remains:

the field flushed white, hills
seduced into bed
by cloud vapor so thin it will

barely last past the break of day,
the trees an erratic screen
against sudden emptiness.

Consumed in association,
their teeth tight to grass,
the livestock nearest the water's

point of clarity absorb this light
in slight movements of jaw and
tongue, slowing the arc of day

as it reaches to nest
in the foreground
of this slowly digested vale.

Tyler Chadwick   93

Field Notes on Language and Kinship

SOMEWHERE IN THE BRUSH
AN ANIMAL STIRS

PART 4: SOMEWHERE IN THE BRUSH AN ANIMAL STIRS

Running one summer evening through the foothills just east of our Pocatello neighborhood, I noticed movement in the loose dirt near the trail's edge. My curiosity piqued, I stopped to see what had scurried across the ground and found a juvenile sagebrush lizard looking back, its legs stiff, holding its body just off the ground, its head and tail cocked—the posture warning me away from its territory. I stooped and regarded the animal for a few minutes, watching its thorax expand and release with each breath, looking at the marks its movement had made in the dirt, and wondering why it hadn't darted into some nearby sage or beneath a rock when I stopped.

I've since considered the possibility that, although its instincts sensed me as a threat and put the lizard into defense mode, the juvenile's inexperience made it curious of my presence. In other words, maybe it didn't run because it didn't yet know any better. Or maybe it was just terrified into immobility. Whatever the case, it barely moved as I slid my fingers through the dirt beneath it and gathered it into my hand. I wanted to take it home because I knew my daughters would be fascinated as I was by its size: head to tail it barely extended beyond by the length of my pinkie. Despite it being so small, though—I hardly felt it in my loosely closed fist—I was keenly aware of its presence as I followed the trail to the road, then followed the road home.

The girls named it T-Bone, although we were never sure if it was female or male; it was too young to sex. For a few months we kept T-Bone in an aquarium in our kitchen, feeding it small crickets from the yard or from a local pet shop until the day we woke to find its body had gone limp. My daughters cried when they discovered it had passed, as I had cried when I was young and found my pet lizards and toads dead. The girls planned a funeral and we had a short service in the backyard, after which I marked the grave with the rock we had placed beneath the heat lamp in T-Bone's aquarium and they went back to playing with their friends.

My encounters with animals, like the one I had with T-Bone, teach me about stewardship, about kinship, about vulnerability and grace, communication and community. I speak to such encounters and the metaphors we sometimes derive from them in this section's entries.

ENTRY 22

While many of J. Kirk Richards' paintings represent moments from Christ's life, a subset of his work depicts landscapes. His paintings of the natural world are just as evocative as his religious work. When I first saw Winter Sunrise, Maury County *(2008), which depicts a sparsely wooded area surrounding a pond, I imagined what animals might be stirring behind the scene and wondered how working with their potential energy might bring life to my words. The result was "On* Winter Sunrise, Maury County *by J. Kirk Richards." My efforts in the poem mirror those made by Lance Larsen, who says in "Why Do You Keep Putting Animals in Your Poems?" (*Fire *257) that when he "open[s] windows to catch a glimpse of grace / on the horizon," animals sneak into the scene and teach him about humanity's presence and place in the world.*

On *Winter Sunrise, Maury County* by J. Kirk Richards

There's nothing spectacular, really,
about morning waiting for light
to seethe into the bark of empty birch,

to ripple the pond just beyond
a twin-based tree, just behind a tuft
of crimson grass, with the arc of day.

But maybe somewhere in the brush
an animal stirs—a squirrel, perhaps, or
a grouse or a housecat lurking

near a mouse nest, instinct taut
against the smell as rich, almost,
as the scene's silence, as full, perhaps,

as God's palate had been when he
trained his brush to subdue this blue
with a careful strain of red.

Tyler Chadwick

ENTRIES 23, 24, & 25

The more I observe and interact with animals, the more curious I become about animal consciousness—about how and what animals think and feel, about how they perceive the world and their relationships to it and to other species. Marilyn Nielson's poem "Sheep" (Fire 310) seems to have been born of similar wonder. In "There was a moment we understood—"I explore how she puts on sheep consciousness in the poem and what effects flow from such empathic performance. "The long notes, impossibly long—"and "As if knowing the exact shade the dead see—"similarly take up and think beyond the human/animal relationship via Lisa Bickmore's "Dog Aria" (Fire 51) and my experience with the death of our family dog. The title phrase of the second reflection comes from Neil Aitken's poem "Burials" (Fire 3) in which Neil uses an experience he had with his late father to explore the nature of death and loss.

There was a moment we understood—

To speak for those who otherwise can't, to give the unvoiced a voice, the other languaged means by which to understand and be understood by others: these seem to be fundamental functions of Christ's mission, at the center of which rests the atonement. In this eternally-in-force act of mediation, Christ descended below and experienced all things in order to enter into relation with all things and so to close the gaps among them—including the gaps inherent in and created by the imperfections of human language and even of inter-species communication.

Marilyn Nielson mirrors this mediatory act in her poem "Sheep" when she gives collective voice to a flock of sheep. Of course, said animals could simply be read as a representation of God's flock—Christ is, after all, the Good Shepherd; and I think such a reading is legitimate. But I also think that reading strips these sheep (as hypothetically actual sheep) of their voice. By making them simply metaphors for humans, we essentially deny them the awe animals must have felt at Christ's birth. Because that's how this poem comes across to me: as a rumination on what it may have been like when the heavenly host appeared to shepherds and praised God the moment Christ came into the world. Surely the sheep must have felt something then, too. He was their Creator and he did come to renew "the heaven and the earth, and all the fulness thereof, both men [sic] and beasts, the fowls of the air, and the fishes of the sea." I'm sure they have some feelings—beyond instinct—on the matter. And they deserve, I think, for us to at least imagine that possibility.

By doing so through her language, by putting on sheepskin and sheep consciousness with her words, Marilyn suggests there may be more to sheep— and by extension, to the lives of animals—than just eating, sleeping, and propagating the species; that there may be more to their experience than just the objects immediately surrounding them; that they, too, may long for "moment[s] / that [hold] more than trees, grass, sky," moments beyond the immediate contexts of instinct and survival. With this suggestion she points to the transformative possibility that the hope made available through Christ's atonement extends to the experience and awareness of animals and that, as we fully enter into a relationship with him, he can also help us understand and perfect our relationship with them.

The long notes, impossibly long—

Lisa Bickmore's "Dog Aria" is about a dog. And not about a dog.

On the surface the poet narrates her dachsund's relationship with water and with song, showing the canine "baying adagio," swimming "among the staves"—the movements of the sprinklers, the dishwasher, the washing machine—as the hush of water grows thick in his ears and baptizes the landscape in night. The friskiness of this image comes through for me in the language the poet uses to frame it: the sibilance of "surprised into song by the slosh of dishes" and the alliteration of "late loads of laundry"; the staccato tapping of "the staccato of his quick sprechgesang"; the playfulness of "Trained in bel canto, he had perfect pitch," which anthropomorphizes the dog and compels a better-trained articulation of the line. If the dog can be trained in bel canto, why can the reader not be trained by the poet to read the poem? This training takes place, to a degree, with the opening of the palate with the long *a* of "trained" and the rhyming short *a*'s of "canto" and "had"; with the alliterative *p*'s of "perfect pitch"; and by the way the line is held together on the tongue with the repeated *t*, a phoneme that's softened and expanded a bit by the *d* of "had" and the *tch* of "pitch."

Below the playfulness of the imagery and the language, however, I sense the poet yearning, perhaps for a deeper relationship with the dog and, by extension, with nature; for a deeper relationship with language; for a deeper relationship with her readers and, by extension, with humanity. This yearning really comes through in "the leitmotif of [the] dog" "and a half," a more-than-animal canine who embodies the poem's deeper themes of kinship and connection. It also comes through in the poem's last two lines: "and the long notes, impossibly long / —O Sigmund! O song!" In her performance of the poem (available on YouTube), Lisa gets a bit more contemplative here and she holds "the long notes" of "long," "impossibly long," and "song" with a bit more longing. Additionally, the two "O"s in the final line signal a lament for the dog, for his song, for deeper kinship with others and the ultimate inability of language to build and to nurture such kinship on its own.

Hence the need for music. Hence the need for poetry, which is language, yes, but also more than language: it's rhythm. It's embodiment. It's longing, kinship, and desire compressed into words, which makes those words more than just mere words.

As if knowing the exact shade the dead see—

After the overdose of anesthesia had cradled Bosley, our almost six-year-old Mini Schnauzer, into his final nap, laying his failing body limp on the vet's toweled exam table, the vet checked his chest for a heartbeat, then looked at me and said, "It's done." She and her nurse left me alone with the body, the door clicking shut as they passed into another room, and I leaned over him and ran my hands over his charcoal coat. As I pulled back the eyebrows hanging long over eyes gone gauzy against the pressure of a brain tumor, I dropped my curtain of tears, leaned in, and kissed the top of his head.

We had noticed the loss of clarity in his pupils just two nights before. Coupled with blood-pooled sclera and his lethargy, head-pawing, and paralyzed jaw—which had come on suddenly about two weeks earlier—we knew something was very wrong. And so did he. Though he didn't have words to say it, I recognize now that he told us in his own way. Just days before we had taken him to the vet where he was diagnosed with trigeminal neuritis. The trigeminal or fifth cranial nerve contains both sensory and motor fibers and is responsible for sensation in the face and certain motor functions like biting, chewing, and swallowing. So he had lost control of his jaw muscles and his mouth hung open all the time; and because his jaw hung open and because the jaw muscles work in relation with the tongue and throat muscles, he had difficulty eating. His tongue lolled heavily, awkwardly when he tried to lick anything and although he could curl it to lap water, he couldn't close his lower jaw so the water would stay in his mouth. What water he tried to drink from his bowl got backwashed and became a gelatinous saliva stew.

The night before the neuritis really set in he wanted more attention than usual. While the family sat together watching a movie, he came to my feet and looked up at me. I could tell he wanted to sit on my lap. He had occasionally done this in the almost six years he was with us, but usually for just a few minutes until he got what attention he wanted and hopped down to make himself a bed elsewhere. That night, though, he slept on me for the duration of the movie. He didn't even stir when our one-year-old came to sit on the other side of my lap—that usually prompted a swift departure. But that night he stayed. And I stroked his curly charcoal coat, wondering what rush of affection had called him to my side.

I know now he was trying to tell me everything wasn't okay, that something was happening inside his head and he didn't quite know what to do about it. I also know that even if he had been able to verbalize this fear, we wouldn't

Tyler Chadwick

have been able to do anything for him either. The tumor was too far advanced for medical intervention to make any difference. So after we got news from the vet that his condition was terminal and he was likely in a great deal of pain, we made the hard—impossibly hard—decision to have him put down. We spent one more night with him at home, with him restless in our bed, and I took him to the vet's office the next morning. They took us back to the exam room and the vet administered a minor sedative to help him relax and then left us. Bosley settled into my side on the chair. I put my hand on his back and stroked him, told him he was a good dog, bit a trough in my tongue for tears. And together we waited out the last minutes of his life.

Two or three weeks later the vet's office called to let us know they had prepared Bosley's remains and we could pick them up anytime. When my wife returned home that day with the sealed plastic container filled with his ashes, I held it for a minute, surprised by its heft, remembering the weight of Bosley's body against my side. Remembering the sudden release I had sensed in him once the anesthesia had taken what control and breath he retained and laid him on the table. Remembering how his eyes got a little bit wider, how they turned toward the sound of my words, how his tongue went lax and slipped from his mouth just before he passed.

ENTRY 26

"When mornings are turned quiet—" speaks to Matthew James Babcock's poem "Moose Remembered" (Fire 13) in which Matt reflects on his memory of a surprise wildlife encounter that shook things up one Saturday morning in his Rexburg, Idaho neighborhood.

When mornings are turned quiet—

Matt Babcock's "Moose Remembered" features a moose, but it's about memory: the redemption of past experience. "This was when," the speaker begins, addressing his wife, I presume, about a Saturday morning earlier in their marriage when he, as a young husband and father trying to make good on those titles, had swaddled their "baby girl" as Mom slept and "carried [the infant] out on the driveway to watch a yearling / moose that had wandered into town from the Teton Basin." He repeats the full opening phrase—"this was when"—once more in the poem; with its third appearance he modifies it slightly, replacing "when" with "everything." In the first two instances, the phrase precedes a statement made in the past progressive: "this was when *we were renting*," "this was when *I was compensating*." This verb construction suggests that the strange confluence of events narrated by the poet was happening when "this" poem, "this" memory, "this" attempt to make himself at one with his personal expectations, his family, his community, and nature were conceived.

In fact, the particular experience narrated in the poem didn't really exist in this form until the poet clothed it in language and breath (something foregrounded by the poem's super-long lines, which take a breath or so to articulate aloud). In that light, this memory *wasn't* until the poet said "this *was*." And the experience gets reshaped—and in the process re-deemed as an important moment (else why record it?)—each time the poem is repeated. Language, then, becomes memory's catalyzing event: as we make and remake the past with acts of narrative, telling others what took place, we form and reform consciousness and lived experience. In other words, human memory grows out of our awareness that we've experienced something worth remembering; and the moment we try to put that something to words is the moment we begin the process of trying to redeem it from the entropy of forgetting.

There also seems to be another attempt at redemption taking place in "Moose Remembered," this one suggested in the third appearance of "This was": "This was everything you missed," the speaker says addressing his wife again in what this time reads as an act of confession. A confession of regret, perhaps, for the delinquencies and other indiscretions that surrounded the family's life-as-remembered in the poem: the rowdy neighbors kept under the watchful eye of law enforcement; the moose running through the neighborhood "like a big awkward kid," a rabble-rousing teenager chased out of town by the same cop who frequented the neighbors' domestic disturbances; the speaker's panicked thinking

Tyler Chadwick

that he had "killed [their] child with / good intentions," even if this involuntary man-slaughter happened only in his head; his being able to give so little to his wife and their baby girl and his subsequent over-compensation for supposedly being so absent as a husband and father.

Once he confesses these transgressions, he seems to find some degree of reconciliation with this confluence of experiences and the people who played roles therein. The morning's "monumental ruckus" dies down. The moose and the cop cruiser slip down the alley beside the movie theater, maybe to play different roles in other memories, to manifest as different desires, different mental policing strategies. Together, the disruptive family next door steps from their house to join the speaker and his daughter in the near-sanctuary of the driveway, where they all enjoy the quiet of communion. And after expending his breath in the long lines of his confession, in the poem's final half-line the poet rests his lungs, his tongue, and his witness of the past because he has fessed up (as it were) to his wife and to himself about the morning's events. And apparently these reconciliations—the ones the poem seems to build up to from the beginning—have, by every indication, been "a long time" coming.

Field Notes on Language and Kinship

ENTRIES 27 & 28

"Green tongues whispering—" and "Desiccated Tongues" respond to the "Adam" section in Michael Hicks' poem "Family Tree" (Fire 218). Both entries began when I first vocalized Michael's poem, shaping its language with my tongue. Its sounds welcomed me into the experience of the poem, which I've tried to understand and extend with my responses. In "Green tongues whispering—" I offer a reading of "Adam"; and in "Desiccated Tongues," I riff off of Michael's language, spinning a lyric engagement of my own with Adam and the serpent. The phrase "desiccated tongues" comes from Jon Ogden's sonnet "Prayer Cap" (Fire 314), which addresses human yearning to commune with God.

Green tongues whispering—

In his poem "Family Tree," Michael Hicks' lines are achingly sparse, haiku-like, even. I find in them a seductive grace and restraint that at once fills me and leaves me wanting. Take, for example, the poem's first section, "Adam":

> The wind hissed
> in the branches,
> green tongues
> whispering
> a secret I could
> never peel open.

As I read it, the sibilance in the first five lines does at least three things: First, it mirrors the layered "hiss" of "branches" and leaves in the "wind," which wind could stand in for the presence of God. Second, it mimics the serpent's hiss and the rasp of its scales against tree bark; this rasp is like "green tongues" speaking to Adam from the knowledge tree. Third, it contracts the tongue and the palate and pulls the lips against the teeth. When combined with so few open vowels— as I sound it, only the *a* in "branches" really feels open—this sibilance forces a performance of the serpent's tongue. By this I mean that it gives readers an experience with the serpent's (Satan's) way of speaking: contracted, meaning Satan holds back some portion of the truth in order to manipulate and deceive others; tight-lipped, implying that he is secretive and bitter; and split-tongued, which suggests he has a duplicitous, sophistic personality.

This closed way of speaking also contributes to the closed nature of the speaker's understanding: he hears a secret repeatedly whispered, but he's kept out of the loop. He can no more "peel open" this secret than the long *o* in "open" (the section's only other open vowel) allows him to really open his vocal apparatus—for a split second, for a passing glimpse behind the secret's veil—before the word closes on him and the sentence and the section come to a full stop. As contractive as this sibilant network of words is, it's also very seductive, teasing me with a sense that there's more to these lines, to these images, that their ultimate secret remains forever open to the reader's interpretive imagination— at least open within the limited system of the poem's language and its kinship with other texts—and thus forever closed to a definitive understanding.

And that's where I leave this reading of "Family Tree": open. Like the sea and the religious canon Moses "split like a log," carving space through which successive dispensations could journey toward deeper kinships with one another and with God. Like Elijah's mouth, once filled with berries by ravens, later a foreboding harbinger of the unmatched power of God. Like the splinter wounds in Christ's flesh, marks mirrored in the true disciple's tongue as s/he praises Christ's passion and sacrifice, which absorbed universal violence and provided means for the establishment of lasting peace. Like Joseph Smith's vision, which set flame to traditional Christianity and, with the ashes, provided fertile ground for the growth of a more sweeping and progressive vision of God, humanity, and our development through eternity.

Desiccated Tongues

Scales hoarse as secrets
whispered between lovers
at dusk, a serpent—and not
a serpent—licks at Adam's
dreams, tasting his flesh
to test what knowledge
had infused the first man in
Father's quickening sigh.

Adam hears voices
from deep in the serpent's
caress, hears a thousand
thousand half-truths split
a thousand thousand tongues
slippery with the blood
of a thousand thousand worlds

before Eve wakes him with
the scent of a half-eaten
quince and a new name
he will only recall in
the half-light between his dreams.

Field Notes on Language and Kinship

EDEN'S HALF-LIGHT

PART 5: EDEN'S HALF-LIGHT

I wrote my master's thesis on the work of Sharon Olds, an American poet who addresses body parts and processes in her poetry without reserve. For instance, in her poem "Monarchs" (as in the Monarch butterfly) she speaks to what seems to be her first lover, reliving what took place during her first time having sex. "No one had ever / touched me before," she says. Then she goes on about her sexual inexperience: about not knowing enough to open her legs and feeling her lover's thighs "feathered with red-gold hairs, / opening" them for her "like a / pair of wings" and about the way her body tore as it opened and left a "hinged print of . . . blood on [his] thighs."

Some readers find Olds' approach indecorous and her content indecent (at least one critic has called it pornographic) and insist that it may be best not to read her poems in mixed company, if at all. I'm convinced, though, that she doesn't go into such detail to shock readers with sensationalism. Rather, like Whitman did with his unabashed confession, "I sing the body electric," Olds celebrates the body (which implies a celebration of sex) in ways meant to startle readers into recognizing and more deeply engaging their physical presence in the world. By confronting readers with language, rhythms, and imagery that reflect and often stimulate the body's natural processes, both poets insist that the body is a vital means of knowing other bodies and of interacting with the world and that to shun sensual experience is to neglect a vital aspect of the soul.

As I read, reread, analyzed, and wrote about Olds' poetry, I gave occasional updates on the project to my wife, who consistently asked me, "As a Mormon, how can you justify reading and writing about sex?" Together, we've thought a lot about that question and what it implies about Mormon culture, which is often quite hush-hush on matters of sex and sexuality, and Mormon theology, which offers an eternally expansive understanding of said matters. Some of my own thinking on the subject has been done in poems and in response to poems and some of those efforts are included in this section.

Tyler Chadwick   117

"*Self portrait with closed eyes,*" *like many of my poems, has a transmedial heritage. It was inspired by and takes its title from a 2000 J. Kirk Richards painting, although the poem's basic form—the self portrait—also converses directly with some self portraits poet Holly Welker has composed (one of which is included in* Fire in the Pasture: "*Self-Portrait as Burnt Offering" [Fire 455–56]). My poem began with Kirk's image in view then spun outward via simile and association into a meditation on Eve and Adam's encounter with the serpent and on the growing physical attraction Eve may have felt for Adam after she partook of the fruit and waited for him to follow suit. Additionally, some of the poem's language began elsewhere. For instance: "desire's simmer / and slow burn" is a direct offshoot of the first line from Mark D. Bennion's poem "Compass" (from his 2009 collection* Psalm & Selah: A Poetic Journey through the Book of Mormon*): "In the simmer and slow furnace / of morning." As I made Mark's words mine via reading and rereading his book, I spun them into something new and wove them into my own work. (Mark's contributions to* Fire *appear on pages 32–40 of the anthology.)*

Self portrait with closed eyes

like a brumal serpent
listening to Earth

shed her crystalline

skin, slip off her chill
at dawn's seductions

supple as hibernacula

warm with bodies
slendering into instinct

and appetite—Eden's

infinite metaphors
sidled up to God's breast,

areola iron on the tongue,

milk rich from desire's simmer
and slow burn, the flame

set low so not to sear the soul

still this side of vision, lurking
like the mourning dove's

anti-climactic elegies

teasing Eve from her
backwoods mythology

heavy with temptation's

Tyler Chadwick   119

pome and tang and the rasp
of cherubim wings strung like

words along Lucifer's tongue

as he conjures shame from
her constant wound—fig

weeping matins in Eden's half-

light while Adam snores
downwind, only stirs when

she's roused scent enough

to slip into his dreams
like the rib slipped from his side

the morning God stopped by

and found the basket of figs
he left last visit

still sitting on the altar,

thrumming with June Bugs
undone in the eating, mad

with the zephyr's rasp

through the scales of the constrictor
stretched at sleeping Adam's side.

Field Notes on Language and Kinship

ENTRY 30

In his poem "Cleave" (Fire 376), Jim Richards poses a series of questions that I don't be-
lieve are fully rhetorical, by which I mean that I don't think he asks them just to make
readers think, but he asks them hoping someone will answer. The second question in his
series comes in the poem's third stanza: "How do we approach the subject / that burns
our mouths like soap?" While Jim never explicitly says what this subject is, it's clear from
the poem's context and imagery that he means sex. By couching the topic in metaphor
(as I've also done in "Self portrait with closed eyes"), Jim suggests that one answer to his
question is that we can approach sex and perhaps better appreciate what it does for human
relationships via the realms of symbolism, where those willing and ready can uncover and
engage its deeper meanings and mysteries.

How do we do *it?*—

Jim Richards' poem "Cleave" begins: "How do we do it / who have never done it before?" I take Jim's "it" to be, yes, sex—but also more than sex. It take it to be the much deeper state of being, the more-than-intimate kinship, the dual state of oneness entered into when partners become more than lovers, lovers more than partners. Such eroticism goes much deeper and means much more than just the mutual pursuit of physical pleasure. Jim ruminates on this impulse in "Cleave," wondering over the ways we can better appreciate the fullness of our bodies and experience a holistic sexuality.

And who is this "we," this collective body in which the poet includes himself? Per line two of the poem: those "who have never done it before." In light of the epigraph of the poem, which comes from Genesis 2:24, I'm going to tack "marriage" onto the end of that thought: those who have never had sex before marriage. Within the Mormon context of the poem—it was written by a Mormon poet and published in *Literature and Belief*, a journal housed at Brigham Young University—I also take this "we" to be not simply pre-marriage virgins, but perhaps a prudish, Puritanical people who may fear the body and its processes and desires and who may further have some cultural history of socially deviant sexuality. I think here of what the poem's speaker calls Mormonism's "pedigree of plural wives," which stretches back, through claims to both God's covenant and literal ancestry, to Abraham and, more recently, through the Church's founder Joseph Smith.

So, how do such people—how do Mormons—do it? How do we learn to negotiate the messiness of it all, the bodies "tangled," to use Jim's word, coming together in such a way that it's difficult to tell where one ends and another begins? "How do we approach the subject / that burns our mouths like soap"? I think the poet means "burns" both literally and figuratively: literally in that sometimes when our kids talk about sex, it's in crude ways that may lead to mouths being washed out with soap; and figuratively in that the subject is holy and, if approached properly, with respect, and in the proper context it can be cleansing, like soap, like fire. How do we approach a subject that we're often told is like playing with fire?

The poet's call-and-response-type poem suggests some answers beyond those I've suggested in this short meditation. Most importantly, however, his use of questions—he does after all leave his inquiry wide open—suggests that we shouldn't shrink from the asking. We need not blush, as a culture or as individuals, when we get curious about the body and its desires. Maybe instead we just need to learn to ask—and to summon the courage to ask—the right questions in the proper context, to consider what these desires mean and where they can carry us and our relationships if approached in the right spirit. As the poet models here, such questions, I think, and such explorations in literature can get us thinking about sex in transformative, redemptive ways.

ENTRIES 31, 32 & 33

In the three entries that follow, I explore the relationship among sex, language, and Mormonism through my exploration of poetry by Will Bishop, Elaine Wright Christensen, and Danny Nelson. I address three stages of sexuality in these responses: "Like passing the sacrament—" takes up the virgin thrill of sex as encountered in Will's poem "When I Do Go On My Honeymoon" (Fire 57), while "Praying for roothold—" speaks to the more mature sexuality that informs Elaine's "Sermon on Manchac Swamp" (Fire 107); "Always the procreant urge—" engages the inherent eroticism of Nature via Danny Nelson's poem "Creation" and speaks to how this eroticism relates to matters of eternal intercourse, which I call the Eros of the Gods. (Danny's contributions to Fire in the Pasture *appear on pages 292–96 of the anthology.)*

Field Notes on Language and Kinship

Like passing the sacrament—

In "When I Do Go On My Honeymoon" Will Bishop captures the thrill—and the anxiety—of embarking on a procreative journey. He begins by engaging a paradox experienced by unsuspecting virgins when they sexually collide atop the marriage bed: a realization that, even though they may intuitively understand the holiness of sex (as the speaker understands it in this poem, at least intellectually), there's more to making married love than turning the "No! No! No!" associated with premarital sex into the "Go! Go! Go!" of marital sex and oiling the mechanics of procreation. Beyond knowing that God ordained sex for our pleasure and for the peopling of the earth; beyond the semantic conversion I mention above and the understanding that Tab A goes into Slot B, the movement into sex-as-sacrament entails an interdependent willingness on the part of sexual partners to embrace the fear of vulnerability.

Will engages this paradox with wonderfully spare lines that mirror the sparseness of emotional vulnerability: "Afraid / but not afraid / to let her touch me," he says, "we'll undress / slowly like / passing the sacrament." This reference to passing, not simply partaking of, the emblems of the Lord's Supper suggests, first, that the pair is acting with God's sanction and, second, that each party's movements are deliberate, meant to prepare the other for the moment of consummation. Such an unselfish and careful approach—literally one full of care—to another's body, even if unconscious, underscores the holiness of sex. Indeed, it emphasizes the very nature of the body as a gift from God, as part and parcel of the soul, which in terms of the LDS cosmology is the union of "the spirit and the body." And, as the speaker reminds us in his closing lines, such a union is a beautiful, pleasurable, ennobling thing: "when I see her body, / bare and beautiful / and not ashamed," he concludes, "I'll kiss her mouth as if / she were the only woman / who ever existed." I'm certain such affection will be returned manyfold.

Praying for roothold—

Ah, "[t]he world is charged with the grandeur of God. / It will flame out, like shining from shook foil; / It gathers to a greatness, like the ooze of oil / Crushed." So Gerard Manley Hopkins, for whom "nature is never spent." For whom creation is a living fountain of ritual, language, rhythm, metaphor—a sensual spring over which the poet moves and "broods" like the "Holy Ghost," spreading his words like his seed, anointing the tongue with lyric balm pressed from the fruits of observation and experience. And so Elaine Christensen, for whom the lyric now—foregrounded in "Sermon on Manchac Swamp" by the repetition of "here"—also consists of moving across waters green with life, spreading language like seed over nascent worlds, anointing the tongue, as the senses, with lyric balm pressed, again, from the fruits of observation and experience.

At least that's one way to read "Sermon on Manchac Swamp": in melodic counterpoint with Hopkins' "God's Grandeur." Indeed, both poems offer highly-textured, deeply-sensual meditations on the pro/creative moment, although each poet approaches that moment from a different angle:

Hopkins goes Grand, ruminating over the Divine Agency—represented in the figure of the Holy Ghost—who oversees and propagates the continual re-creation of a "bent world" "trod" and "trod" and "trod"—all-around taken advantage of—by humanity's "generations"; a world "seared with trade," scorched in the process of exchange between bodies, "smeared" and "smudge[d]" by their inter-relational "toil" and, like those bodies, "smell[ing]" of human sweat.

And Elaine goes local, focusing "here," on a particular experience with particular flora and fauna in a particular geographical location—Manchac Swamp, Louisiana. In her verbal performance of her poem (available on YouTube), she even reads the poem with local flavor, though not the Cajun-spiced palate you might expect from a poem come out of a Louisiana bayou; rather, her performance tastes very much like Wasatch Front Utah. Her tone is sincere and endearing, her inflection attitudinally positive, her facial expressions emphatic. She is no staid Modernist or metaphysical poet. She is rather a bit Relief Society, a performance register that tends toward didacticism and sentimentality.

This very Mormon register provides an interesting contrast to the deeply sensual imagery of Elaine's poem, which is far from didactic and sentimental. It's ultimately erotic, after all, beginning with its post-pubescent setting:

an aging swamp matted with "Spanish moss" "crisp and wiry" as pubic hair. The scene sets up a meditation on mature sexuality: "Here" where "lean[ing]" "cypress" yearn to maintain "roothold," to remain erect, potent, vital. "Here" where bodies smolder in "wet" "heat," where schools of fish "hang / just below the surface," rising, perhaps, only on rare occasions. "Here" where the poet and her companion "listen" to maturity's "sermon on / idleness," on simply being with another body, basking in "how it smells" (a mark of physiological attraction), "how it smiles" (emotional attraction), and in the "immense satisfaction" of riding the soul's vessel with another "happily into the shade" of mature sexuality.

Yes, indeed, the world—including the body—is charged, erotically and otherwise, with the grandeur of God. And that is a deeply religious, deeply spiritual, deeply poetic proposition.

Tyler Chadwick

Always the procreant urge—

Danny Nelson's poem "Creation" remixes the Old Testament's opening text. In so doing, it delves deeply into the "procreant urge of creation," a phrase straight out of Whitman's celebratory "Song of Myself." Indeed, in "Creation," as in Whitman—and, I would argue, most poetry—I sense the "Urge and urge and urge, / Always the procreant urge of the world." This impulse toward connection calls "opposite equals"—such as poets and readers, females and males—"out of the dimness" of matter unorganized into bodies and relationships eternally on the verge of Being or greater manifestations thereof. Danny captures this paired advancement in his poem with its depiction of the creative union of the sun and the moon, an interaction that represents the male and female aspects of Nature working together to weave a new sphere from the fabric of the universe.

Within the Mormon context of the poem (it originally appeared in *The Fob Bible*, a multi-genre anthology composed by a writing group made of Mormons of various stripes), the creative movement of these opposite equal spheres further implies the eternal creative and procreative influence of both male and female Deities over the universe. For if we have a Father in Heaven and if, as Eliza R. Snow reminds us, "truth is reason," then, she continues, "truth eternal / Tells me I've a Mother there"—and that she's doing more than merely keeping House. Rather, as Danny's variation on this theme suggests, she, as represented in the creative power of the moon—which during the earth's creation "lifted land" from the watery void, "set the rain in silver sheets / upon the ocean's stormy streets" and placed "birds in flight" and fish in the sea—and as the feminine coeval with God the Father, is an active participant in the eternal, reiterative round of creation. And her presence in this eternal pairing makes creation's circling dance more productive of all that is good, beautiful, and holy than many of us may care to—or even, at present, can—imagine.

But that doesn't mean we can't or shouldn't try to imagine what such a relationship might look like or to consider the extent of its influence in or on our existence. I find this especially true when I think of humanity's procreative companionships, which, if we believe what Joseph Smith taught, are simply mortal reflections of the "sociality" of the exalted: those beings "*coupled* with eternal glory." I take "coupled" here to mean at least three things: one, exalted beings are inextricably linked to the glory of God, whose name is Eternal; two, exalted beings are paired as Eternal husband and wife within the highest "order of the priesthood [meaning the new and everlasting covenant of marriage]"; and three, such glory and order, such Eternal kinship, necessarily includes acts of sexual communion, which are not meant solely as the means to propagate the Gods' genes—as "a continuation of the [pair's] seeds"—though that is, of course, a necessary function of the coupling. Rather, such an eternally-interdependent union of opposites deifies the procreant urge such that this impulse continues, deepens, and tempers our inherently human passions, making them as Eternal as God, whose well of emotion runs deep as eternity, as is evident in the breadth and depth of emotions he expresses in his interactions with humans: anger, anguish, sadness, happiness, joy, a fullness of love. I'm convinced that such divine love encompasses—is even heavily informed by—God's procreative power. As Book of Mormon prophet Nephi testified, even though he didn't "know the meaning of all things," he knew "that [God] loveth his children": the fruits of his eternally procreative body.

Though this matter of eternal intercourse—the Eros of the Gods—is essentially, as Brigham Young taught, "a hard matter [for us] to reach" because "it is without beginning of days and end of years" and so, ultimately, beyond the limits of mortal comprehension, we can, as Brother Brigham continues, "tell some things with regard to it." And what can we tell? That "it lays the foundation for worlds, for angels, and for the Gods; for intelligent beings to be crowned with glory, immortality, and eternal lives. In fact it is the thread which runs from the beginning to the end of the holy Gospel of Salvation . . .; it is from eternity to eternity." This thread thus not only links the procreative pair to one another and to God in Eternal matrimonial bonds, it further binds them to the Gospel of Christ and to the expansive range of God's creation. In this way, Eros is ultimately the catalyzing force in the universe. It can draw together and renew bodies in a sacramental bond that nourishes the soul. Such eternal eroticism—as a deep expression of eternal love and kinship mirrored in our own sexual coupling—nourishes us and our relationships. It can lead to the "continuation of . . . lives" because it encourages fully empathic connections to other bodies. And it does so in ways that move us beyond the flesh into service to another's corporeal desires and that drive us to create and procreate: to leave our personal mark on the universe, a tendency many poets acknowledge (though not always explicitly in sexual terms) in their efforts to re-imagine familiar worlds and familiar words, as Danny has done with "Creation."

ENTRY 34

At its root, an essay is a trial, an attempt. It's a place to weigh things out, to test and develop ideas, to experiment with words. From this noun comes the verb "to assay." In "'I Took This to Mean': Poetry's Communal Moment and the Virtues of Textual Intimacy," I assay my encounters with Latter-day Saint sexual mores, with poetry as a communal act rooted in the body and in kinship among bodies, and with Mormon theology's expansive view of embodiment, procreation, and desire. In the process, I weigh these encounters against my readerly desires, my family relationships, and my experience with specific poems by American poets Lucille Clifton, Sharon Olds, Walt Whitman, Allen Ginsberg, and Javen Tanner (Fire 430–31). The result is a mosaic in which I've tried to let each idea, each poem, each relationship cast light on the others and to show how these influences have shaped my understanding of the relationship among eroticism, language, and literature.

"I Took This to Mean": Poetry's Communal Moment and the Virtues of Textual Intimacy

As a Mormon since birth, I grew up in a religious tradition that maintains strict taboos on matters of sex and sexuality. Because of these taboos, many Latter-day Saints eschew talking about sex. In fact, Church members are often counseled that even to think about sex is a sin. Such counsel is based on Christ's teachings from the Sermon on the Mount, which he reiterated in a sermon given to his Nephite disciples in the ancient Americas. In both he warns that to lustfully consider another person's body is tantamount to committing sexual sin; it's also, as he cautioned early nineteenth-century Mormons, a denial of faith in him and of his Faith (meaning his Church). As such, it leads to spiritual death, to being cut off from communion with God through the Holy Ghost. Because of this, he continues in his sermon to the Nephites, we should deny ourselves the dangers of lustful thinking by casting such thoughts from our minds before they can kindle our physical desires. Otherwise, our desires left unchecked will damn us. From this perspective on morality, it follows that, lest we're seeking damnation, we should not only avoid thinking about sex, but anything *like unto* thinking about sex. Among other things, this "like unto" category may include such intellectual infidelities as reading about sex—an act that could invite into the mind whatever lusts a narrative describes or might arouse in readers—as well as contemplating the reading process itself as an inherently erotic act of intercourse between a writer and a reader.

Because I had been raised into this moral perspective, it pricked me with shame, embarrassment, and guilt when as a young, married graduate student I developed an interest in the ways gender, sexuality, and the body are represented in literature. Before that I had stifled the attraction for a time, doing my best to put from my mind what stories I had read for college assignments that addressed one aspect or another of the human sexual experience. I even recall having once condemned a professor—though not to his face, mind you—because he made us students read a poem that at the time I considered immoral. It was called "lorena" by American poet Lucille Clifton and it referenced the story of Lorena Bobbitt, who in 1993 was raped by her husband, John Wayne, so she cut off his penis and threw it into a field. Everyone in the class was familiar with the story. But when the professor gave us the poem and had us read it during class, he withheld the poet's name and the poem's telltale title to see if we could still guess its subject and meaning. The activity was intended to help us understand the ways knowledge of a text's title and author influence how we receive and interpret the text. The poem begins, "it lay in my hand," then slips into a meditation on the nature of authority: how it can shape a person's being. I remember thinking how sensitive the poem was, how softly it held its subject in hand before letting it go. I forget, though, any guesses I made regarding what the poem's "it" was. Those were lost when the professor revealed the title and I realized what I had been handling as I attended so closely to the text. In the aftermath of his revelation I felt repulsed and vulnerable, which made the poem seem less beautiful, more crass, more macabre—and completely tasteless.

It took years after my encounter with "lorena" before I could move beyond my initial revulsion and think differently about the poem—actually, before I even returned to think about it at all. During the interim, however, I encountered and was tutored by the work of Sharon Olds, another American poet. In her poetry Olds unabashedly—some would say gratuitously—explores the body and its functions (far more than Clifton does in "lorena," in fact). Whether she's addressing the press and tear and rush of childbirth, the ripening adolescent body, the thrill of attraction, the ecstasy and release of intercourse, the slow burn of maturing desire, or the flesh hanging doughy with age, she rarely holds back or euphemizes. For instance, in her poem "The Language of the Brag" she exults in the exceptionality and heroism of childbirth. As she does so, she bares her flesh and the acts and products of her flesh, exposing herself to readers and to the poem's addressees as if to a delivery room full of strangers whom she has gathered to witness her feat of endurance and strength. Imposing her blood-washed newborn on this audience, she presents the "new person" as the exceptional fruit of her "exceptional heroic body," holding up the acts that produced this fruit as being "epic" and, as such, worthy—by far—of sustained attention.

The word *epic* derives from the ancient Greek adjective *epikos*, from the noun *epos*, which means word, story, or poem. Etymologically speaking, then, something that's epic is something that deserves the attention of language. In terms of literary form, an epic is a long poem that narrates the heroic journeys and deeds of a protagonist whose life and character exemplify the values of the poem's originating society. Epic poems were traditionally composed orally before a live audience who had gathered to experience or to re-experience the hero's adventures (I say *re-experience* because many listeners would have been familiar with the legends and story cycles around which the poet wove his particular narrative). Giving the event varying degrees of attention and receptivity and moving with the crowd vicariously through the hero's adventures, listeners could participate with the poet in the story's creation and elaboration. In the process, depending on how much attention listeners gave and how receptive they were, they could also likely feel the poet's language deeply, viscerally, as his voice washed over the crowd and resounded with their flesh, exciting the passions and evoking the senses' response. In these cultural circumstances, poetry and the process by which it was made were shared by the community and rooted in the connection among poets' and listeners' bodies. During poetry's communal moments, which enacted the essential kinship between poets and listeners, both parties in the transaction may have had their individual and communal values and desires both validated and kept in check as, through the performance event, they mutually recognized and committed to emulate the hero's strengths and learned how not to be via the hero's shortcomings. In this way poetry traditionally functioned as a physically offered and physically received means by which community members might gain shared experience and might confirm and maintain individual and communal values and desires.

Olds' use of the term "epic" in "The Language of the Brag" calls upon this function, especially as it was adapted and used by two American poets: Walt Whitman and Allen Ginsberg, both of whom she directly addresses in her poem. In the mid-nineteenth century, Whitman set out to establish as epic everyday Americans performing everyday deeds. He did so by creating a new verse form that was bound up in his breath and in the rhythms of his body and of the changing American landscape and that asserted his experience and desires as the pantheon of American selfhood. Hence the opening line of his long poem "Song of Myself," where he asserts, "I celebrate myself, and sing myself." That he intends readers to experience at his side the poem's narrative journey to increased self-understanding is apparent in the next two lines, whose additive structure ("and . . . for . . .") binds them directly to the opening statement: "And what I assume you shall assume, / For every atom belonging to me as good belongs to you." I take this to mean that he believes readers should want to take on—to assume—whatever characteristics or personae or expressive forms he takes on in his lyric journey because these atoms, these building blocks of American being, belong to whoever—like Whitman—will claim and embody them.

One such expressive form is the "barbaric yawp," as Whitman calls it, or as Olds names it, the "proud American boast": an unrestrained voicing of pride in individual accomplishment and desire. Adopting this form in their writing, Whitman boasts about a self-concept that encompasses America—the land and its people—and Olds about the fruits of her self-described exceptional body.

Ginsberg, in a similarly expressive act, titled his best-known yawp "Howl," a sprawling poem whose breath-length lines fill the page with visions of individual desire and the pursuit thereof as manifest in the social turmoil of mid-twentieth century America. "I saw the best minds of my generation," Ginsberg famously begins, "destroyed by madness, starving hysterical naked, / dragging themselves through the negro streets at dawn looking for an angry fix." The poem brims with such images of exceptional passions pent up by repressive social structures to the point of hysteria and seeking release. Hence Ginsberg's rant, which names and seeks to counteract the effects of repression. The poem's counteractive agency becomes most apparent when it's potent language is voiced, an act that purges the emotions in the poem and in the reader and listeners and that, long line after long line, repeatedly empties the reader's lungs, which exhalation in turn decreases the heartrate. The additive effect of these performance processes serves, among other things, to relieve the psyche, to relax the body, to clarify the mind-body connection in the reader and in listeners, and by so doing to call the physical desires into the conscious mind where those desires can more readily influence and be influenced by language.

The epic function of Ginsberg's howl—as of Whitman's yawp and Olds' boast—grows out of such sustained intercourse among poet, reader, listener, and language: an exchange given and received via the body. For all three of these poets, in fact, there doesn't seem to be much more worth giving sustained attention to or boasting about than the potency of individual bodies and their potential to come together and produce new bodies, new stories, new social circumstances, new worlds. All three seem to assume the workings of this relationship in the way their poems are composed—with language, imagery, and rhythms rooted in the body and meant to call forth and influence readers'/listeners' desires. Olds even depicts the interaction directly in "The Language of the Brag" when she places her speaker at the center of a crowd whom she addresses and makes demands on with an expression of her body. And though Olds' poem is far shorter than either Whitman's or Ginsberg's and can't be considered epic in terms of literary form, her expressive act—the body she created with, pressed from, and boasts about via her own body—demands the designation "epic" because its creation and introduction into the world were communal, heroic acts and its journey through the world, where it may perform or participate in similar acts, will be, the speaker implies, just as communal and heroic. In this light, the processes by which bodies propagate—including sex, conception, gestation, contraction, and the spill of a mother's water, feces, and blood

Field Notes on Language and Kinship

during delivery—demand consideration as both physical acts and as metaphors for acts of human kinship.

I didn't, of course, come to this realization after just one encounter with Olds' work. It took many sustained encounters during which my understanding developed as does the protagonist's change in any good story: out of experience and reflection and conflict. Which means that I not only read literature my Mormon sense of morality cautioned me to avoid—literature like Clifton's "lorena" and much of Olds' or Whitman's or Ginsberg's oeuvre—but I studied it, considering especially its contexts and implications. As I did so, though, Mormonism's sexual mores pricked me with shame and anxiety such that I continually questioned the source and object of my interest. Was I simply rebelling against the morality I had been taught since childhood? Or did my intellectual desires and my proclivities for textual interpretation have redeeming value? I hoped it was the latter and sensed there may be virtue in my efforts. Still, as a youth I had been taught (as young Mormons are still taught) not to even think about sex and to only do things I would be comfortable doing in the presence of my parents. Based on the habits of thinking I developed in the wake of these teachings, I couldn't help but wonder: What would my parents think if they knew I was spending time with poems that talked about sex? What would they say if they discovered I was noticing and writing about the sexual imagery latent in narrative art? How would they react if they learned I was taking great intellectual pleasure in my reading, writing, and thinking about sex and literature? Because I was exhilarated—and didn't think I should be—when I began exploring a subject that I had been led to believe was intellectually off limits and that I had been taught to simply put out of mind.

At first my indulgence in the pleasure of texts felt illicit, like I was cheating on my religious tradition. So I carried the affair on in secret, confining myself to a silent room as I read and wrote because I had extended the counsel I received as a youth to include my wife, Jess, and our daughters and (perhaps naïvely) considered my family's presence a medium of surveillance and judgment. It was a reminder that my heritage of Mormon morality (in the guise of my parents) was always looking over my shoulder, silently taking notes on my thoughts, my words, and my behavior—and what's more, that these notes, as the Book of Mormon prophet Alma suggests, would ultimately condemn me. But slipping away for short periods from these figures of cultural surveillance (at least as I had configured them in my head), I felt I could let my guard down and give way to a text's rhetorical caress: to the influence of language and sound over mind and body. My slipping away was often literal as I sought quiet places to read. Even more often, though—and this included times when I had settled into a quiet place—it meant slipping into a reading persona I had constructed to separate myself from my inner conflict and to cope with the disparities between my burgeoning readerly desires and my Mormon sexual inheritance.

I say that I constructed the reading persona, but that statement assumes deliberate action: that I played a conscious role in the persona's creation. Rather, it came into being as my psyche brooded over the silence of my indulgence and drew from that morass of conflicting desires material with which to shape a character whose readerly sensibilities were beyond the purview of Mormon cultural surveillance as I perceived it and that as such were unaffected by the conflict I was experiencing. This persona had deep faith in the virtues of textual intimacy, particularly in the kinship bonds we can forge with others when we engage narratives that don't shy away from the human sexual experience, when we tease the latent sexual imagery out of other narratives, or when we give ourselves over to a writer's rhetorical caress. His faith in these virtues stemmed in part from his faith in and love of language, a passion that made him at once playful with words—if at times adolescent—and deeply concerned with how words function within and influence the world and, especially, with how they influenced him.

As he gave more and more of himself to this passion, engaging with texts when he wasn't attending to other obligations (and sometimes when he was or should have been attending to other obligations), he realized how much his encounters were being shaped by his family relationships, including by the excitement he saw in his young daughters as they mimicked his interactions with language. Because they saw him carrying around books, notebooks, pens, and pencils—things he often left piled around the house—they took an early interest in the tools we use to make the written word and packed them around, too. It delighted him to watch each girl play at reading and writing and he was invigorated by the openness with which they played. Even though the nascent sensual and intellectual desires pulsing through their flesh were, like their handwriting and the scribbled notes they left laying around the house—in the kitchen, the hallway, the bedrooms—still embryonic, unrefined, indiscriminate, they had no reason to hide them or to be self-conscious about them. The girls were, after all, quite young and hadn't yet been socialized into the Mormon cultural mores that would bring them guilt or prompt them to guile in such pursuits and compel them, as it had compelled me, to cover their tracks, to subdue desire's bloom with the regulatory lexicon of Latter-day Saint morality.

In addition to the influence his daughters' burgeoning intercourse with the written word had on his own intercourse with language and narrative, this persona's desires toward his wife shaped his encounters with texts. The intimacy and the kinship bonds they shared became touchstones for him as he slipped beneath cover of language to explore the flesh behind words, to trace skin ripe with intention and passion and vulnerability to his textual delight. I'm not saying that he exploited this relationship to construct unwholesome sexual fantasies from the materials he read. Neither am I suggesting that he wanted to hop into bed with every pretty or witty text he picked up online or at the library. What I am saying, though, is that his marriage, which freed him to direct his physical desires toward his wife, also gave him language and experience that helped him to keep those desires in check by considering them in context: as part of a covenant relationship in which both partners offer each other their total being—physical, emotional, intellectual, and spiritual—in a process that binds lovers together with an abiding sense of loyalty and trust, that prompts each to attend to the other's desires and needs, and that moves them both in pursuit of shared purpose and pleasure.

Based on the understanding he developed via his marriage relationship and that he shared with his wife, before he would yield to what pleasure a text promised, he looked for more than just linguistic chemistry. He needed to know there was more beneath the words than just a ripened textual body or the free flow of passion and consciousness and the desire to connect, to commune, to procreate—to know and be known by the world. He needed more than rhetorical foreplay to encourage him to give way to another textual body. Indeed, because he understood that there's more to language than mere erotics and more to eroticism than just sex, he lived by an ethics of textual intimacy that allowed him to enter into deep kinship with a text and to maintain his moral standards. And while his erotic morality might seem somewhat paradoxical, especially in light of his virginal, ultra-chaste Mormon upbringing, his textual ethics couldn't really be separated from this Mormonness. His faith in Mormon teachings about the body, sex, and sexuality, in fact, ultimately bred his conviction that sensual experience, like the still waters of the twenty-third Psalm, can be sacramental to the soul.

The presence of this figure's third-person pronoun in my mind was liberating.

Tyler Chadwick   139

Even though I wasn't aware of his company at first, his whispered suggestions allowed me to think beyond—to transgress—the limits of my Mormon sexual heritage and to embrace a Latter-day Saint theology of desire. Whereas the former often seeks to sweep sex and sexuality under the cultural rug, the latter provides an eternally expansive view of the subject. As I've noted elsewhere, such a theology is founded on the principles of eternal eroticism and encompasses the gods' creative yearnings and procreative relationships—their eternal couplings—and the fruits thereof: their offspring and other creations and the sense of responsibility they bear for these fruits. In this sense, LDS doctrine ultimately proposes that erotic desire binds procreative partners to one another, to God, to the fount of his love, and to the expansive range of his creations; and this line of reasoning further suggests that Eros is the catalyzing force in the universe. It draws together and renews bodies in sacramental bonds that nourish the soul. Having been convinced of these truth claims, my reading persona felt no shame, as I did, thinking about sex and sexuality in the presence of our shared moral legacy.

As my awareness of this persona grew and I learned to read through his eyes, to understand the theology of desire, and to be comfortable with increasing levels of textual intimacy, I became more willing and able to seek deeper kinship with others through the acts of language and narrative. With this increased willingness and readerly ability came the desire to reconsider texts I had previously treated carelessly, texts that I had brushed off because, at first glance, I thought them immoral. I returned, for instance, to "lorena." After my first encounter with the poem had ended in revulsion, I walked from the classroom condemning both the poem and the professor who forced it upon me. When I had shared the experience later that evening with Jess and her parents, they validated my judgment: "How inappropriate!" they said, after which they added, "Couldn't he have chosen a better poem?" Revisiting their response years later in the guise of my persona, I realized how their language reinforced the reading values that flow from Mormon culture's strict sense of morality. Since they hadn't read "lorena," I thought, and couldn't have been aware of its aesthetic qualities, their modifier ("better") must have been directed at the moral quality of Clifton's text—or rather at its apparent lack of moral quality. Their assessment, which was based solely on my secondhand account of the classroom activity, implied that other texts were inherently the poem's moral superiors. As such, these texts, by virtue of their virtue, deserved sustained attention while Clifton's morally inferior poem did not. What's more, my family members' question assumed that my professor shared our Mormon system of morals and that his choices were motivated by that system. Yet, he didn't and they weren't—but we didn't consider that at the time. Instead, we were convinced that his decision to share with the class a morally suspect text was an affront to virtue and an abuse of his and his students' agency and his authority as a teacher. Hence the declarative, "How inappropriate!," which had reinforced our sense of Mormon morality and in the process condemned both "lorena" and the professor's decision to impose the poem on his students.

Reconsidering these assumptions in the light of retrospection, however, I recognized how they also reiterated to my subconscious the influence my family members had over me as cultural surveillants, unsuspecting as they were that they filled this role. The more time I spent in the guise of my reading persona, though, the more he began to overshadow these figures as they were constructed in my mind. So instead of the agents of guilt and shame whom I had once imagined peering judgmentally over my shoulder, taking note of my readerly indiscretions, I now had someone at my side who fed my readerly desires by encouraging me not to dismiss out of hand texts I would have once thought immoral but to first consider the potential virtue of those texts: to hear them on their own terms, to understand their character, to reflect on what influence they might be trying to exert on the world.

His presence changed my response to "lorena," whose appeal had been lost when I learned that the poem addressed a penis—as if the subject matter automatically made Clifton's language less virtuous and her manner less sensitive (although knowledge of the subject does add dark humor to the narrative). When I revisited the poem in search of its virtue, I was drawn in by Clifton's approach: she slips into Lorena's experience by speaking from Lorena's narrative point-of-view: "it lay in my palm," she begins. By using the first-person pronoun instead of the third-person, Clifton hones in on the immediacy of Lorena's act and refuses to distance herself or her readers from the violence it represents, which is how the more distant phrasing "it lay in her palm" would have functioned. This choice of pronouns makes her better able to explore—and to exploit—the symbolism of John Wayne's severed member. By so speaking, she holds out to readers the social function of this metonym for masculinity and male power. Because that's how the penis-as-symbol functions: as a socially-constructed metonym. As the channel for distribution of male seed and therefore as the primary measure of a man's physical potency, in many societies the penis stands in for all assertions of male power and authority. In fact, many men rely on aggressive

Tyler Chadwick

sexuality and sexual acts to dominate others. From this perspective, to cut off the male organ is to strip a man of his power; indeed to even question the male organ, whether as a flesh-and-blood appendage or as a symbol of male potency, is to sow seeds of doubt in the bedrock of male influence. Hence what Clifton does with "lorena": speaking from the frustrated woman's perspective, she meditates on the authority assumed and the promises made by her subject (as an actual object and as a symbol): how like saints and angels it would elevate to heaven—it would make fly—both the man and those who yielded to his desires. Then she lets it fall to the ground, showing its ultimate failure to deliver by suggesting that, although she and her society may have attributed the penis divine sanction, the appendage-as-metonym is inherently flesh-bound and fallible. Leaving her subject at readers' feet, she challenges those who will listen to become aware of and to end their complicity in the cultural performances and institutions that perpetuate and aggrandize male authority. A worthy response would include, I think, questioning and seeking to revise acts of language that assume a man's sexual potency is an inherent measure of or entitlement to social and/or divine authority.

Yielding to the character of Clifton's language lured me into Lorena's experience (and the implications thereof) as mediated by the poem: into the helplessness that must have driven her to violence against her husband. Into the vulnerability she must have sensed in him and his body and that she must have relished as she cupped his severed member in hand, contemplated it a moment, then threw it into a field. Meeting "lorena" on these terms convinced me that there's nothing suspect about the poem's morals, that it's actually deeply empathic and seeks to stir others to compassion for and kinship with the abused and to social action against violence. Both Clifton's poem and Lorena's desperate lashing out did this for me, evoking the weight of my responsibilities as a husband and a father of daughters, especially, but also as a writer and a teacher: someone committed to studying and sharing with others the virtue of words, which have the power to profoundly influence our minds, lives, and relationships. In fact, taken together the acts of these women convinced me, as I had been convinced before and have been further convinced since, that one of the most effective ways I can establish and strengthen kinship bonds is not by trying to control others—whether by physical, emotional, or rhetorical violence, all of which severely limit the receiver's potential to act—but by stirring their desires and seeking to commune with them, to create new possibilities with them, to jointly compose open-ended stories with powerfully made language.

Although my reading persona wasn't exactly me, I recognized enough of myself and my desires in him to know that he had been constructed from the materials of my life, that he was one of the many possible iterations of selfhood that my mind could have made from my experiences, relationships, and habits of being. As a version of me who wasn't quite me but who I could potentially become, I also recognized him as a coping mechanism: a story my subconscious began telling when it sensed a conflict between what I had learned from Mormon culture about sex and how my desires were being tutored by both the literature I read (and took great pleasure in reading) and the LDS theology of desire as I understood it and felt it mirrored in my marriage. These influences came together and I consciously began taking control of the story—moving the persona from his relatively distant (and thus less risky) place at my shoulder into my skin—when I first encountered and began pursuing a relationship with Javen Tanner's "Eden" (*Fire* 430–31), the opening poem of Javen's 2006 chapbook *Curses for Your Sake*.

"Eden" addresses and seeks to enact in readers the kinship bonds we can forge with others through acts of physical and textual intimacy. The poem opens at a dinner party where the speaker isn't fulfilled by the "proxies" of "satisfaction" he finds there—"guests, food, chatter"—and he longs for something more, something that can take him beyond temporary and superficial acts of human kinship, beyond gastronomic appetite and delight, beyond the idle and incessant flow of meaningless conversation. "And then," he says, just as his yearning surfaces in a string of disjointed words, "*she* was at my side." Taken with the poem's title, this sudden appearance alludes to and remixes the Biblical moment when Adam awoke from God-induced sleep to find Eve at his side—his rib, his bosom companion, bone of his bones, and flesh of his flesh. Javen's remix of the mythology begins as the woman speaks: "Meet me in the garden," she says. Her appeal functions on at least two levels, one figurative, the other more literal, though in terms of this poem neither can really be separated from the other. On the literal level (or at least to be taken literally within the realm of literature), I would expect any reenactment of Eden to take place in a garden: a space separate from the busy-ness of civilization. What's more, the narrative ought to engage representatives of Adam and Eve in a struggle to understand relationships among material and spiritual bodies, male and female, good and evil, human and divine. Javen's depiction is no different: shortly after the woman requests the speaker's presence outside, he anxiously enters the garden. Waiting for her to join him, though, he's distracted by "the laughter from the house, / the ruinous clatter of dishes, / / the air sick with warm sugar" as it settles around him, drifting outside through an open door or window.

Adding the figurative level to the woman's request deepens the dramatic effect of this setting, giving the poem's Edenic mythology a greater sense of immediacy. The speaker makes this move to the figurative when he interprets the woman's invitation to meet her in the garden: "I took this to mean," he says, *"Come with me / and we will be buried in water, / fire, nomenclature, earth."* The double entendre implied in the phrase "Come with me" suggests not only that the speaker understands the woman's desire to meet, but that desire is the reason for the meeting and that the mutual fulfillment of sexual desire may consummate the pair's encounter. To be buried in this sensuous pleasure, to be immersed in the rush of hormones and fluids, the passion, and the deep kinship of sexual intercourse is to enter a ritually-enacted relationship between bodies that serves as the source and metaphor for broader connections among material and immaterial entities across time and space. For sex is more than pleasure, more than passion—though it is those, too. Sex is also sacrament: a primal generative and regenerative ritual meant to unite physical bodies in the propagation of the species and shared invigoration of the flesh.

Speaking to the intersection of poetry and human passion in terms of Sharon Olds' work, poet Alicia Ostriker suggests that the "impulse to connect" bodies manifests a human need "to perceive unities across the conventional boundaries" that separate such bodies—whether they be words, lovers, and generations; flesh, psyche, and spirit; subject and object, artist and viewer, poet and reader. As a natural extension of this line of thinking, she further submits that any effort made to satisfy this need is "always implicitly erotic, always a form a making love." In other words, the urge to bring bodies together in creative relationships is a function and manifestation of our sexual desires and our procreative needs. Javen's speaker seems to agree, as implied in his interpretation of the woman's invitation to meet. His statement uses metonymy to make associations between the impulse to connect bodies—to form and to consummate kinship bonds—and other acts of communion. These include human sexual relationships, through which bodies come to pleasure together and fulfill mutual desires in moments of deep vulnerability; religious ceremonies, like baptism by water and by fire, through which we seek to build and sustain a relationship with God; human language use, through which we name our relationships and commune with others through narrative acts; and death, through which flesh rejoins earth. In the speaker's system of meaning, then, sexual fulfillment, religious rituals, language, and death stand in, respectively, for the fullness and the fruits of satisfying kinship bonds, for the potentially redemptive influence of religion, for the mind- and world-shaping influence of words, and for the consummate union of flesh and universe.

With these metonymic relationships in mind and with the poem's lyric voice—its union of word, sound, rhythm, and sense—pulsing through my body as I verbalize Javen's words, when the woman says, "You've come" after she appears in the garden "under the heavy shadow // of a peach tree," I sense myself slip more fully into the drama of the poem. I feel this presence keenly when I speak the stress placed on "come," then pause at the period's full stop. Having reached the climax of her statement, I experience the declarative as a consummation of the voices sharing the encounter: the poet's, the speaker's, the woman's, mine. Such interplay among rhetorical bodies bears fruit: in terms of "Eden" and its conjugation of voices, the heavily shadowed "peach tree" becomes a pregnant "shadow" or type for the woman's sexually mature body. When considered with the poem's setting, this body further represents and is an offshoot from the knowledge tree, whose ripened fruit welcomed Eve then Adam into the fullness of embodied experience. The speaker's interpretation of the woman's declarative suggests what this fullness might entail: that the bonds made by lovers will multiply their sorrow, "spread serpents" at their heels, "spit curses" for their sake. I take his catalogue of effects to mean that the closeness of kinship will function in at least the following ways: it will cause lovers to feel deeply into each others' lives, to experience each others' sorrows and ecstasies, and to be expanded in the process. It will serve as a source of antagonism and redemption in lovers' lives, the serpent being a widely-regarded symbol for both Satan (the Great Antagonist) and Christ. It will initiate and represent uses of language that can be both deeply destructive (i.e., full of curses) and deeply reparative (i.e., made for our sake).

"Eden" represents well the paradoxes inherent in making and honoring deep kinship bonds. Once the poem's speaker has catalogued the promises of embodied experience, his attention turns from the woman's declarative to the fruit whose scent emanates from her hands. In the economy of their kinship this fruit is, he observes, at once "forbidden and necessary": forbidden because, like her body, he can't partake of it until she offers it to him. He can observe it from a distance, but out of respect for her being he can't touch it, can't taste without her permission. And the fruit is necessary because, also like her body, it makes demands on him physically, emotionally, mentally, and spiritually. Its declaration of being—which it speaks simply by being present in the world—invites and entices him to meet the woman on common ground, to join her in the mutual pursuit of purpose and pleasure, to be and to become with her. In this sense it's the key to unlocking the fullness of their individual and joint potential, to consummating the promise of their kinship bonds.

As I read "Eden," this consummation comes in the poem's last four stanzas. With his attention directed at the fruit in the woman's hands, the speaker hears a door open. Through that fissure into a world apart from the garden, a voice—perhaps God's, perhaps a party guest's, perhaps both—calls his name, teasing him with this very specifically directed word to join her/him inside. But the speaker refuses the invitation—"once, twice, gone"—choosing instead to stay with the woman, whose ripeness seeps through the narrative just as the peach she splits drips juice into her hand. I've sensed a rise in this pheremonic tide from the beginning of the poem in the alliterative dance that increasingly lingers on the ridge between my lips and my palate, as when the woman "split the peach" then "licked nectar / from her fingers, // and said, 'Here, taste.'" Reading these lines, it's all I can do not to taste the sounds as they caress my tongue until meaning explodes from the friction among the words, the lines, my breath, and my mouth in the poem's last two stanzas.

The speaker initiates such rhetorical procreation by revisiting the role vulnerability and interpretation play in acts of intimacy, whether textual or otherwise. After the woman speaks for the third time in their encounter, saying "Here, taste" as she offers him juice from her fingers, he says, "I took this to mean," a repetition of the phrase he offered in response to her first two statements. I take this echo as a reiteration of poetry's communal moment: when a listener yields to the influence a poet's language exerts over body and mind and, through this influence, enters the drama of a poem, making her/himself vulnerable to its textual body and the meanings it calls forth. In the case of "Eden," the poem's speaker gives way to the woman's words and allows them to rouse meaning from his desires, morals, and experience. A step further away from the narrative, I've taken the speaker's cue and submitted to the influence of the poet's words, receiving them as I would a flesh and blood body: reading and interpreting their cues to help me experience, understand, and respond to the poem's full textuality. Because the poem's body is full—as in ripe, as in complete—in that it embodies both halves of a procreative whole. Not only do both its female and male characters speak but its language bursts with an array of articulative poses that manifest poetry's procreative disposition: its potential as a highly compressed and kinetic literary form to seed in a reader's body and mind new bodies and new worlds, to author with a reader new relationships through the subtle movements made within a text. Or alternately, because I recognize the maleness of my verbs (to seed is to inseminate, to author is to father): poetry's potential, as a fertile vessel of language and experience, to birth new bodies, new worlds, new relationships as conceived during communal moments with readers and to nurture these materials into newborn rhetorical realities.

The interplay between these potentialities is especially apparent in the last two stanzas of "Eden," in the imagery and phonetics of the speaker's concluding statement. After speaking his reiterated phrase, he riffs off of the woman's directive that he taste the fruit she holds out to him: "I took this to mean," he says, "*Here is my heart, / delicious and desirable. / See how it beats and bleeds,*" he continues, "*how it breaks to heal itself.*" His interpretation of the woman's words makes full use of a dynamic range of sounds and articulative poses. He begins on an *h*, which occurs in the statement more than any other consonant and which is productive at various points in the mouth, creating friction at each place it's performed in the vocal apparatus. With *here* and *heal* it presses air between the tongue and the section of the hard palate just behind the alveolar ridge; but with *heart* and *how* this occurs farther back, at the soft palate. The movement of this voiceless fricative (as it's called) holds the statement together, alliterating to highlight the statement's two central terms, *heart* and *heal*, which the rest of the expression modifies. The heart, the speaker says, is delicious and desirable: an object enticing to others' interest and senses. The adjectives enact this allure; and as suggested by the fact that they've been given their own line, they deserve close attention: the lush consonants that linger on the tip of the tongue—the word-ending sounds, especially—then spill into the directive to "see," which in turn briefly opens the palate before the bilabial implosions of "beats," "bleeds," and "breaks" release what tension remains in the poem and resolve into its closing phrase.

The implosive verbs of the final sentence both reflect and describe the heart's agency: as a bodily organ it beats and bleeds; metaphorically, it can break. And to what end does it function in these ways? To heal itself. For instance, the more the heart works, the stronger it becomes and the better it can feed and rejuvenate the flesh. But if the organ weakens, the system breaks down. The heart's role in maintaining itself and its body's health carries over into its vitality as a metaphor. Consider this in light of the following: to get at the heart of a matter is to uncover the thing's essence, its true nature; and to say that someone has heart is to ascribe them depth of character and desire that won't allow them to abandon their goals, no matter the obstacle. What's more, to give someone your heart is to offer them your deepest self, to reveal to them your innermost desires, intentions, and tendencies. As these illustrations suggest, the heart as a metaphor represents the most vital and vulnerable part of a thing; just as failure of the actual organ will devastate the body, if the heart were to fail in any of these circumstances, the breakdown would bring them to ruin. Neglecting the heart of a matter denies its true nature and can lead those guilty of neglect to misunderstanding, conflict, and delusion. Losing heart equates with giving up and giving way to the lie that the sustained pursuit of goals is a mark of flawed character. And having someone reject your heart is akin to them rejecting you and can lead to a sense that you're inherently broken and deserve to be disregarded like a mis-manufactured toy. Thereafter the choice to extend yourself to others takes on greater risk: to be so vulnerable, so exposed would put the self in danger of dissolution. It would open the heart to being broken.

But without risking the broken heart, without extending ourselves to others, we can't enjoy the pleasures or the promise of intimacy, which is what the woman offers the speaker in "Eden" and what the poet offers readers with his language so lush with desire: an invitation to intimacy. As I accept his invitation by submitting to the power and influence the words on the page exert over my mind, my body, my heart, soul, and words; by slipping beneath cover of language and making myself vulnerable to the textual body, reading its cues and shaping my response accordingly, my physical and psychological rhythms explode into meaning. And a new text is born of the matter between us: a rhetorical offspring conceived during poetry's communal moment. From this particular encounter with "Eden," it was this text; from another encounter, it may be another. Whatever the case, I'm more and more convinced that the nature of my textual relationships derives from how much of myself I'm willing to divulge during moments of textual intimacy; and the more I'm willing to give, the deeper the well of communion runs. Hence my slipping among memories, among words, my wrestling beneath cover of language, trying to keep the cultural Mormon in me from damning myself for being so sensual: because I'm convinced that there's virtue in giving way to the material that binds us as human communities—to shared morals, to mutual passion, to language and deep bonds of kinship.

So I extend my hand through the veil of words.

Take it however you will.

Field Notes on Language and Kinship

BETHESDA

PART 6: BETHESDA

Just north of the temple block in ancient Jerusalem there was a pool called Bethesda, which is Hebrew for house of grace or house of mercy. Hemmed in by five porticos, this space, like a womb, gave shelter, hope, and a new beginning to masses of the infirm—the blind, the lame, the leprous, etc.—all of whom gathered to wait for what John the Beloved called the troubling of the water. As the folk story goes, the intermittent agitation of the pool was the result of an angel's touch, a repeated moment of divine intervention that gave the water curative properties, which would pass to the first body that entered the pool after it moved.

Each time the water stirred it disrupted the crowd grown stagnant with flesh-rot and waiting as the poolside population contended for that single spot in the waves. The competition clearly favored the most able-bodied in the group, or at least those who were attended by able-bodies—those whose increased mobility allowed them to slip unaided into grace. Which left the least able-bodied—those perhaps most in need of the water's balm—to settle back into their husks of filth and disgrace to wait for their next chance at a miracle.

In "Back, back to the beginning—" I speak to my own curative pool, my center, my Bethesda when I say that my family's presence in my life troubles the brooding waters of my soul. By which I mean that the demands they make on me emotionally, mentally, physically, and spiritually are an angel's touch. They disrupt me from complacency and self-interest and insist that I become a more capable, more compassionate, more engaged human being. Their constant presence in my thoughts also makes demands on my language, influencing deeply the ways I think about words and stories and how they function in the course of everyday activities and relationships. I address some of those demands in this section.

ENTRY 35

In "Giving the Beauty of Holiness a Tongue" *I explore the demands family kinships can have on our language. The essay responds to Doug Talley's 2011 book* Adam's Dream: Poems for a Latter Day *and was originally written as a book review for the Association for Mormon Letters. (Doug's contributions to* Fire in the Pasture *appear on pages xi and 425–29 of the anthology.)*

Giving the Beauty of Holiness a Tongue

I.

On an anxious night in my mid-teens, I knelt bedside, my soul full of fire and forgetting. I don't recall the exact cause of my anxiety—just that it sprang from my puzzling, as many teenagers do, over an uncertain future. And this puzzling had led me to prayer, which came out that night as nothing more than indistinct yearnings pressed from the soil of my breast like seedlings just breaking through. I imagine they barely tickled God's ears. But he must have been listening more articulately than I was speaking. At the moment my yearnings were ready to coil back upon themselves, his language swelled the soil around their roots. Or it might be more accurate to say that his stillness, like water, welled up in the ground of my soul, flowing from somewhere deep in his center to quench my anxieties enough to let the language of my experience speak. When I was still enough to listen, a proverb of Solomon, which I had read a few weeks earlier, flooded my consciousness: "Trust in the Lord with all thine heart and lean not unto thine own understanding. In all thy ways acknowledge him and he shall direct thy paths." Since that night, I've returned often to this stream of words. I've paced its shores, hoping the obsessive repetition would purge me of anxieties. I've plucked stones from its bed. I've rolled them in hand. I've skipped them across the surfaces of God.

One such return took place during the fourth month of my wife's first pregnancy when she started spotting. Startled by her yell from the bathroom where she had been getting ready for work, I ran from the kitchen and met her halfway down the short apartment hall. "What should I do?" she asked, absently handing me her crimson-brown spotted undergarments as she turned, without waiting for my response, to call her obstetrician. While she spoke with her OB, I slipped into the bedroom and knelt beside the bed. Wringing the undergarments in my hands, I churned them in the proverb's stream, telling God the bare-bones of our situation: our first child, four months along, my wife suddenly spotting please oh please oh please let everything be okay

Just as I've left that sentence open, I'm not sure I ever closed my prayer. But everything turned out okay, with both mother and child, our anxieties notwithstanding.

While I'm confident our oldest daughter would still be with us even if I hadn't offered my inarticulate petition to God, I'm not sure I would have learned what I did from the experience if I hadn't hit my knees and at least tried to verbalize my desires. (Not that I'm saying God set the circumstances in motion in order to teach me a lesson, just that the lesson arose out of the experience.) As I lingered on the banks of that prayer, waiting for my anxiety to settle, I flipped open the scriptures that were sitting beside me on the bedstand. They settled on Malachi 3, parts of which I had memorized in my LDS seminary classes and which had come up in nearly every LDS Sunday School or Priesthood lesson and sacrament meeting talk I had ever heard on tithing. So I was familiar with the refrain: "Bring ye all the tithes into the storehouse . . . and prove me now herewith, saith the Lord of hosts, if I will not open you the windows of heaven, and pour you out a blessing, that there shall not be room enough to receive it."

The language that really seeped into my soul, though, was this statement a few lines down the page: "neither shall your vine cast her fruit before the time in the field." Until that moment I had never associated my young family's corporeal prosperity—which right then centered in my wife's reproductive health—with the blessings of tithe-paying. But as I let Micah's words wash over me that morning, I sensed that our meager young-couple offerings were accepted by God and that the fruit of my wife's and my procreative bodies would not be "cast" from the womb prematurely.

I don't pretend to understand why, even among God's faithful, some pregnancies reach full-term and others miscarry or result in stillbirths or why some couples have no trouble conceiving while others never can. But I am convinced a) that God heard my clumsy pleas that morning and somehow appended them to the other prayers that had been, were being, and would be offered for the blessing of my family's generations; and b) that my oldest daughter is a great blessing to our immediate and extended family.

II.
The power of honest language (even if it's clumsy) offered to God on the altar of humility is cumulative. It extends well beyond the range of each individual voice raised in prayer and joins with other voices that express similar desires across time and space. It even extends beyond the limits of the specific words used in prayer and the capacity of the supplicant to use them. Brigham Young acknowledged as much in a sermon delivered to a group of saints at Box Elder, Utah, June 7, 1860. Speaking to the fruits of discipleship, he observed, "In praying, though a person's words be few and awkwardly expressed, if the heart is pure before God, that prayer will avail more than the eloquence of a Cicero."

After all, he continued, "What does the Lord, the Father of us all, care about our mode of expression? The simple, honest heart is of more avail with the Lord than all the pomp, pride, splendor, and eloquence produced by men." In Brother Brigham's economy of worship, then, the clumsy, fervent prayer is more effectual than the well-wrought, yet dispassionate one.

Plato leveled a similar argument against the traveling teachers known as the Sophists in Ancient Greece, suggesting that the Sophists' eloquent mode of expression was mere "flattery" and "personal adornment" and that Truth (capital "T") was not to be found in pursuits associated with the use of mere words. I sometimes sense this same distrust of language in contemporary Latter-day Saint culture. In a sacrament meeting talk I once heard (as in many others), the speaker mentioned how much s/he admired a certain leader because this leader was a man of action, not words. Instead of talking about what needed to be done, he just did it. Imagine, this speaker seemed to be saying, it we talked less about service and just served.

While there's certainly merit to this attitude—after all, as the adage goes, actions may speak louder than words—what about those saints for whom words are a matter of faith, which is a principle of action and of power and thus one means of providing service to others? What about those who successfully combine the simple, honest heart with an eloquent tongue, those who are convinced that words act upon and influence the world and our existence in and relationship to it in profound ways?

This is one of the central arguments of Doug Talley's 2011 poetry collection, *Adam's Dream: Poems for a Latter Day*. In this collection Doug weaves his experience and desires as a husband, father, and son into hymns, parables, prayers, and lyric meditations on the kinships among humans and between humans and God. In the process, he revisits metaphors and narrative forms we often use to describe, to understand, and to commune with God and his kingdom. Doug thereby takes up language as a form of worship—meaning that he not only uses his poems to *praise* God, but also to *emulate* God, whose words create worlds out of chaotic matter.

If we think of poetry in etymological terms, as I think Doug would have us consider it—*poesis* being the Greek term for the process of making—God is the first Poet. And Adam was his apprentice. It was Adam who first built an altar from which to approach the heavens in the true order of prayer and it was Adam who named the animals and cultivated the earth, bringing order to a fallen existence. Doug has also entered this apprenticeship; and with *Adam's Dream* he has crafted an altar of words around which we might gather as he translates the language of angels into an extended, eloquent, fervent prayer that our souls and our families might be touched and transformed by the simple beauties and the language of holiness.

III.

Adam's Dream is divided into four sections: "Land within Arm's Reach," "Temples Framed by Hand," "Voices from Another Room," and "Flowers of a Kiss." Each section contains eighteen poems and is framed by a nineteenth. These frame poems unfold one line at a time throughout each section, with a new line appearing in the header of each page on which a new poem begins. When taken together these extra poems serve as an extended, four-part prayer, as suggested by the final of these four parts—the extra poem that appears in the section titled "Flowers of a Kiss." (In order to maintain the associative power of this selection, I've left off the end punctuation because in the book each line appears followed only by an ellipsis):

> The autumnal decline resigns the spirit
> Yet beauty remains a daily commonplace
> As ironies swarm like dark stars and haunt
> Songs of the spirit will answer need in the smallest particular
> Spirit and flesh join as equal tutors of belief
> In covenant after the manner of stars and flowers
> The two are made one
> As type and shadow of a resurrection
> The heavens open in more ways than one
> Eternity courses time like a thread of words
> A few key words remain, even as the flower fades
> Culminating in further illumination at the veil
> Words and gestures of faith resound through all generations of time
> Until even the harshest irony surrenders
> One word above all others
> Circumscribed in one eternal round
> A woman shall compass a man
> With no beginning and no end
> in the name of Christ Jesus, Amen.

Each part of this petition could arguably take the section heading beneath which it appears as its title, though each could also just as easily be unnamed. Whatever the case, Doug veils his book with this poem-prayer in all its associative glory, a veil through which he reaches in order to gather readers around the altar of linguistic worship where he drops words like live coals on the tongue. Among other reasons he does this because, as he observes in his Foreword to the book, "The beauty of holiness begs a tongue"—and with his lyric gifts and his prayer he sets out to share and to prepare readers to receive and to express that beauty lingually.

In this light, consider the book's opening poem, which appears beneath the following statement—the first line of the first section's extra poem: "In an early light the beauty of holiness is manifest," which suggests the innate relationship between holiness and light. The poem is titled "Hymn of the Morning Star":

> Morning spreads across the sky.
> Birds begin to sing.
> Their voices raise our thoughts of praise
> to Thee, our God and King.
>
> Who else gave the sparrow breath?
> Crocus its blue song?
> Or gave us choice to add our voice
> in worship all day long?
>
> Who but Thee, O Lord, our God,
> nurtures each good seed
> and answers prayer with patient care
> according to our need?
>
> Give to us an angel's bread,
> though a crumb or trace,
> and then we'll sing an offering
> as with an angel's grace.

With this intricately arranged opening hymn, Doug not only mirrors in his book the structure of most LDS worship services—which typically begin with a hymn—but he offers a fitting invocation to his collection.

Tyler Chadwick

The connection between singing and praying is clear enough, especially in Mormon culture. As the Lord told Emma Smith in 1830 when he called her to compile a book of hymns: "my soul delighteth in the song of the heart; yea, the song of the righteous is a prayer unto me, and it shall be answered with a blessing upon their heads." And the connection between poetry—especially lyric poetry—and singing is also fairly clear. In his *Defense of Poetry* (written in 1821 and published in 1840), Percy Bysshe Shelley observes that "A poet is a nightingale, who sits in darkness and sings to cheer its own solitude with sweet sounds; his [sic] auditors are as men entranced by the melody of an unseen musician, who feel that they are moved and softened, yet know not whence or why." In "Hymn of the Morning Star," Doug draws both connections, suggesting that as he and his fellow poets "begin to sing[,] / Their voices raise our [desires and] thoughts of praise / to . . . God." Framed in this way, the poet becomes an intermediary figure, one who might sincerely and eloquently sing in order to "move and soften" others, including, perhaps, God.

In *Adam's Dream* Doug sings a variety of songs, leading a multivoiced chorus of lyric meditations on and mediations for the world. Among others, this chorus of fellow poets includes: God, Adam, Matthew, Mark, Luke, John, Dante, Vergil, Horace, Shakespeare, William Stafford, Doug's kids. This multivocality is apparent in one of my favorite poems from the collection, "Latter-day Aesthetic" (*Fire* 429). The poem begins, "I once had a dream I was William Stafford / riding a bicycle to China to become a poet." Not only does the poet slip into the guise of another person in his dream, he also does it in this poem by taking on something of Stafford's own "natural mode of speech," which American poet James Dickey describes as being "gentle, mystical, half-mocking and highly personal daydreaming about the western United States." Within the shadow of this mystical/playful/personal voice and, in Doug's words, "encouraged by the views of an oriental sage / cycling alongside [him] with the same ambition," the poet plays with the fiscal advice proffered by this muse—"In China, he said, you make good living as poet"—and spins it into an exploration of what makes poetry a means to living well. "True or not," he says of the sage's bit of fortune cookie wisdom,

we were entirely content, happy

to chase on a bicycle our dream in a dream.
What was it but a voice from another room,

a whispered oracle from some templed vision,
a truly original idea perhaps? I think of Adam,

the first in so many things, tending red peonies
in a garden, the first man to laugh, the first

to reach for a woman with love instead of lust,
the first to use words as metaphor and symbol.

Perhaps I was the first to dream of crossing
the Pacific on a bicycle in the guise of another

—a simple, animated descendent of the first
of all true originals—led from the brink of hell

to the fringes of heaven on a wave of ocean
flamed by sun and moon, believing all the while

a poem must sparkle like water for the soul
in creating the world, or prove nothing at all.

Beyond suggesting that poetry can help us live deeply and well by engaging us with language and imagery that ignite the imagination to conceive of new dreams and to reach for and to inhabit other worlds and other words, "Latter-day Aesthetic" also argues for the poem as sacrament, as "water for the soul." Doug fully realizes this aesthetic communion in "Perspective on Greater Eternities." In this poem he "consider[s] the great cities of the earth, / how each from the air appears set like a jewel" in Earth's crust, and how Christ refused this "handful of baubles" when Satan offered it to him "in the mount." To each of Satan's temptations Christ had responded by referring to something an earlier prophet had spoken. "It is written," he said, reaffirming what Doug calls "a few, old words" and "reshuffling" them in the new context "into loaves of bread": into sacramental language that would someday feed generations of God's children and raise them into holier, immortal flesh.

Flesh and blood, body and spirit, the sacred and the commonplace, heaven and earth, man and woman, the language of worship and everyday speech: these are paired terms Doug juxtaposes, explores, and combines throughout *Adam's Dream* and through which he seeks to resolve the ironies of mortality—or at least to ease the burdens imposed on us by them. I think of one poem in particular that is drenched in irony and whose imagery is drenched in iron: "Parable for the Pulse of the Wrist" (*Fire* 426). In this lyric narrative, Doug recites a story he's fond of telling and retelling, because, he says, "I never tire of its strange beauty, / its happy ending returning over and over to smile at me." The story:

> One bleak winter evening a good doctor deftly cut
> the umbilical cord wrapped three times around the neck
> of my firstborn to save her from strangling to death.
> An intern noted the moment precisely, seven past seven,
> because, like a garden hose suddenly gushing water,
> the cord, once severed, whipped a circle of blood
>
> halfway across the room against a pale yellow wall,
> against the blue scrubs of those standing by the bed,
> against the face of a clock fixed at seven past seven.
> The splatter of blood on glass could have been a chime,
> a red stripe announcing its own peculiar name for the hour.

The irony of the poem centers on the fact that blood had to be shed in order for Doug's firstborn child to survive delivery, a bloodshed beyond that which may typically accompany childbirth. He draws a parallel between this blood sprayed across a delivery room and the blood shed by Christ in Gethsemane. With this parallel and his extended meditation on it, Doug suggests that, yes, childbirth and its antecedents—procreation and pregnancy, especially—are acts of atonement, ones that send the mother deep into the valley of death so she might give life to her child. He also suggests that these acts and their associated ironies can—as the iron (the blood) that whipped across everyone and everything in his story—give life to more than just the child. They can also tutor the belief of an anxious mother and father. They can return a little bit of innocence to the world. They can course through time like and in response to the thread of words strung in effectual prayer among and for a family's generations.

ENTRY 36

"For the Sycamore" was inspired by J. Kirk Richards' 2001 painting Zaccheus, *which in turn led me to the story in the Gospel of Luke that inspired the painting: Zaccheus descending on Christ from a sycamore tree. Kirk depicts their interaction from a distance, shrouding them and the crowd come to hear Christ in shadows. Four figures in the image captured my interest the first time I saw it: Christ, whose hand, in silhouette, points to Zaccheus; Zaccheus, whose pose partly mirrors Christ's; and the mother and child positioned in the painting's foreground. The angle of Zaccheus' arms point directly at the pair, whose presence alludes to Mary holding a newborn Christ. So: Christ points to Zaccheus, who both reflects Christ and points to a mother and child, who in turn allude to Christ and his mother. This compositional relationship set my path in "For the Sycamore," which, as I described in the Introduction, hadn't felt complete until I added to the final stanza a line from N. Colwell Snell's "Vienna 1965" (*Fire *388).*

For the Sycamore

She's always been the narrative crux,
her branches grown thick
as his presence in Luke, him raising
his faith so he can anoint God's head
with his sweat, her shadow pinned tight
to the Teller's canopied bosom of words.

She's no different here in her browns
and rusts, peering down the blouse
of my soul from the artist's throng,
playing my gaze through the spaces
among her sprawling geography.
She frames her fruit well on that throne

of a branch where he sits mid-startle
against the plot twist, holding his perch
to keep from falling too hard
on his faith. Yet the centuries
nearest her act, the children of the children
of the child nearest the viewing pane—

see how she tilts her head toward the throng,
mouth wide; tries to suckle
from the tale—forget; even Zaccheus
moves on after Christ points him out, calls him
down, invites himself over for tea
with the publican and his family.

But Christ's finger reaches
beyond his words, beyond pigment, beyond
the curving branch of the sycamore
he touches at last. Always
to the Garden. To the serpent. And
Eve, knowledge gnawing at her lips

Tyler Chadwick   163

like juice pressed from a thousand figs
(how could she not savor every drop?)
as Adam walked in from the cool of day
and she reached to fit his waist
with the apron
she had learned to make from her Mom.

ENTRIES 37 & 38

In their poems "Inheritance" (Fire 400) and "Legacy" (Fire 141), Sally Stratford and Danielle Beazer Dubrasky (respectively) explore the relationship between grandmother and granddaughter. The way an older generation shares stories with a younger generation is central to both poems. I respond to Sally and Danielle's stories in "I want her to wake up and tell me stories—" and "Still thirsting for milk—."

I want her to wake up and tell me stories—

The most striking thing to me about Sally Stratford's poem "Inheritance" are the images that suggest being clothed/covered/dressed in one's legacy, that imply, in Sally's words, how we can "wear [a] name" that has been passed between generations. There's the "two carat diamond / which, like a heavy rock of salt, / falls to the side between [the speaker's] fingers," an image that suggests the precious nature of a heritage that doesn't quite fit. There's the grandmother's "skin loose / like pie crust draping over apples." This skin, or rather the DNA that like the art of baking an apple pie, is something passed between parent and child. There's "the green sequined dress" the speaker's grandmother once "wore to the country club," which looked "like a waterfall of thin emeralds." This bejeweled garment becomes at once symbolic of the need to fit into one's legacy, but doing it in our own way, even when others—including parents or spouse—may suggest otherwise. There's the grandmother's bed, which will "soon be empty, / the electric blanket smooth / over her place," both objects that, like the warmth of the woman's legacy, provide some degree of comfort to the speaker. And finally, there are "the reading glasses on the [bed] table," suggestive that this mother has left behind a particular way of reading the world, one inherently captured in the poet's life and stories.

The confluence of these flowing images of fabric, jewelry, apple pies, and skin occurs in line ten, where the speaker laments, "I want her to wake up and tell me stories." Narrative, in whatever shape and form, is the way we order the world. It's really what makes us human: we use words to tell stories, to gather our loved ones around us, to share our memories. And it's the structure of language—the subtle connections among words (rhythms, rhymes, spacing, etc.)—that holds this poem together because in all its elegiac longing, the thing that keeps it from spinning into unrestrained grief at the speaker's potential loss are its subtle internal rhymes, its alliteration, its meter.

These connections are what drive me back to poetry, to narrative, to language. They're the things that hold us together even as we threaten, in the face of the postmodern loss of faith in language, to spin out of control. But there is power in language to bind us in kinships that exist beyond words. And as Sally's poem demonstrates, this is an essential part of our human inheritance.

Tyler Chadwick

Still thirsting for milk—

In Danielle Beazer Dubrasky's sonnet "Legacy," Danielle explores an intergenerational relationship—and the rippling effects thereof—among three women and one man: the poet, the poet's grandmother, the grandmother's brother, and the poet's great-grandmother. This complex relationship is narrated from the poet's point of view as she observes her grandmother's interactions with her material, maternal heritage. Grandma carries this heritage in her habits of being—her characteristic ways of interacting with the world: in the "afghans" she knit and the "roses" she cultivates and that perhaps she learned to cultivate by watching her mother care for her own garden. These objects "give her day a pattern." And through the routine tasks that make up this daily pattern, she can focus her failing energies and channel away any undercurrents of resentment that threaten to disrupt the placid surface of daily living.

But the violence done her in the past manifests in her present emotional and physical state. When the memory resurfaces of having been emotionally and physically neglected by her mother in favor of "the favored son"—who got fattened with milk because, apparently, "only boys needed calcium, not girls"—the resentment builds up and "her mouth purse[s]." The emotional force of such pursing is mirrored in the vocal force required to speak the word purse: notice the explosive release of breath and sound that bursts through the bilabial *p* and that is slightly suppressed by the *s*. The poet's grandma represses such emotional explosion with her daily routine—but only partially. That she's still bitter—and deeply so—comes out in the linguistic friction present in Danielle's retelling of the memory, especially in this phrase, "how her mother would fatten the favored son," and in the imitative reiteration of Great-Grandma's claim ("only boys needed calcium"), which likely remains with the daughter because it was perhaps too often repeated.

Yet, bad memories, destructive language, and bitterness aren't the only holdovers from childhood neglect. There was also physical and relational damage done. As Grandma explains through the poet, "She gave me weak bones"—and someone to blame for an inadequate skeleton. I also surmise that she got a strained relationship with her brother out of the deal, a brother whose dated gift, the "Dresden shepherdess"—a substitute for his presence in her life and his attempt, marked by the doll's "milk-white" skirt, to maybe make up for what he got that she didn't—darkens with the physical and psychic space she inhabits as autumn permeates her world. In this space, she, as perhaps the poet, longs to redeem that little girl still "thirsting for milk." They long to give her language with which she might recover what she lost, if not in bone structure, then in the psycho-emotional scaffolding of a healthy intergenerational relationship, one built on compassion and the desire to connect intimately, empathetically, with another flawed and frustrated, trampled over soul.

ENTRY 39

When I completed "Mother & Child" in 2010, the poem had been in the making for nine years. It began in 2001 during a phone conversation I had with my second oldest sister, Tiffany, in which I announced that Jess and I were expecting our first daughter. Tiffany took the news hard because she and her husband had been trying several years for kids without success. She told us congratulations but her honest response to my announcement snuck through the line before my other sister, Taryn, whose phone I had called (they were out shopping together), could hang up: "That makes me so mad," she said. Her statement stuck with me and became the catalyst for several iterations of the poem I wanted to write about Tiffany's experience.

That poem didn't happen until late 2009 after another phone conversation with Tiffany. During this one she shared news that they were going to adopt a little boy. Our lives had come full circle and the experience wanted to be told, though it still took some time before I found the right language to tell it. That was inspired by another of J. Kirk Richards' paintings, this one part of series of Mary and Christ images titled Mother and Child. I was particularly drawn to the one subtitled (Yellow)—painted in 2001—in which Mary and Christ emerge from and fill out a geometrical pattern. The composition's geometry gave me my opening lines and the rest developed from there.

My poem converses with others that appear in Fire in the Pasture and that depict women holding children as types of Mary holding Christ, both in his infancy and his death. These include Melissa Dalton-Bradford's "Pietà" (130), Deja Earley's "I Teach Six-year-Olds about Jesus in Sunday School" (157), and Will Reger's "Mass Transit Madonna" (373).

Field Notes on Language and Kinship

Mother & Child

1.
A matter of geometry, these two:
mother and son bisecting desire,
trilling between syllables of miracle
on the insatiate tip of God's tongue,
plotting points of spirit-cum-body-cum-
solitude across the palate of this
Cartesian life.

                    Like Euclid pictured
space, cropped it tight, then pinned it
to his wall. Dressed the plane's blank stare
with theorems intersecting as bodies
at birth, flesh strung on strands
of one-point-six-one-eight: golden ratio
flung, lasso-like, from Gabriel's tongue
around Mary's vestal flame. Around
Elisabeth's reproach:

                              a woman
kneeling bedside, telling tissues
wrung dry as a rosary run out of beads.
As her uterus chapped like a mid-drought
riverbed: no rain to replenish
the abyss. No rain to bed dust stirred
by mourning doves' grief. No rain to
tune her divining rod to God's promises.

2. After the in vitro
fell through, she laughed with Sarah,
patron saint of laughing at God's vows,
through deprivation's bearing down.
Birthed one grand guffaw as Sarah
brushed hope like dust from
a ninety-year womb, strung motes
of desire on golden strands, then
willed her the rosary. Suggested

Tyler Chadwick   171

she hold tight the umbilical, telling
its folds until God gave in, said he would
trade her maternity for that altar of a laugh
she had knelt at ten years, stained month
after month with grief's insatiate memory.

3.
The morning she rang with her adoption news—
late-teenage birth-mother, boy due in a month,
and her: without crib, clothes, blankets;
her guestroom of a nursery barely
broken in beyond a few days' hospitality—
the annunciation half-raptured, half-
stalled through the line. As if she
thought the angel divining her son
from that womb of a crystal ball
would say, "He's yours," fingers crossed
behind the vow.
                        Not that I blame
her hesitation: Subtract seven years from
that minor denouement and you've got
the elegy she hyphenated upon hearing
we were pregnant: "That-makes-me-so-mad."
Meaning, "Cruel logic, this: sibling mathematics.
Three years I've squared flesh
by my husband's flesh. Primed numbers
with an actuary's acumen. And
all I get? Endometriosis divided by
infertility's stigma in the State
of 'So, How Many Kids?' While they
slipped out of contraception a month
and, voilà, fruit the size of my desire.
God? That-makes-me-so-mad."

I never told her I heard her post-benediction
more-petition-than-expletive. Never
confessed that her brooding slipped
through as she turned from my call

to refuge in wrath equals grief equals
me, holding the dial-tone seven years.
Counting the absence beneath her words
like abacus beads. Keeping track
of the meter until she could shape
her next line around, "He's mine."
Breath compressed, released, caressed
across the palate to relief:

                    Zackary.
Zackary. Name moist enough to tame
the cowlick thick, like hers,
across his pate. Enough to swaddle him
to sleep the first night—and the second,
third, fourth, fifth—he cozied into the hollow
worn beneath her breast by infertility's slow
drip (gnawing constant as incontinent pipes
up ten years with the pinch) and slept. Slipped
in and out of infancy while she traced his
fingers tight as rosary beads across
his palm, *Amen*-ed, counted again. More
slowly then, as she timed her body to his:
his rise, fall, rise against her slight repose.
As she mapped his subtle topography
into the golden bloom of dawn.

Tyler Chadwick

ENTRY 40

"Pater Noster" responds to J. Kirk Richards' 2010 series of forty small portraits of Christ, all of which depict Christ's face only in gesture (like sketches in paint). The poem also converses with Arwen Taylor's "Lingua Doctrinae" (Fire 444–45), which plays, as my poem plays, with the language of worship.

Pater Noster

i. Litany

Ah! to, snakelike, tongue
your subtle psaltery. To

taste your staves profane
as the Gloria Patris

tonguing my cheek,
tonguing the irresistible,

iron-rich canker I've
mapped like a bad habit,

traced and retraced
like a compass rose

etched in the mouth's
wilderness. To tell

faces sketched
from memories remembered

sidelong, laid down on
lambskin scraps strung

like shrunken heads
on God's rosary, features

fingered dull through
a Sibyl's aeon spent

stroking the omniscience
she inherited from her folks.

Tyler Chadwick

To lip the oracles you've
lipped like live coals

passed in God's palm
to purge the palate.

To savor how her Verb
verbs everything else,

how
her cleft-tongued hymn

seers everything else.

ii.
Scratch that: *sears*. Like

the conversation kindled
backstage memory.

The one you can't help
eavesdropping on, pressing

your ear to a glass pressed
to the partition you raised

to keep the noise down.
Next door, a chorus

incants oracles from
the soul's velum. But all

you hear is the string
of blasphemies you let

slip from your dreams
just before you wake.

Field Notes on Language and Kinship

iii.
No. Not blasphemies:
God's image stripped bare,

retrofitted with words
pinched from the dove's

dictionary, etymologies
shat on the water's face,

turned spindrift, pronounced,
Elegy. Movement. Desire.

Grace. Breaths skipped
while you translate

the body's pieties into
stones pale and smooth

as faces waiting,
waiting to be named.

iv.
Like the pebbles
my two-year-old

plucked (and repeat)
plucked (and repeat)

plucked (and repeat)
from stones pooled

in the feral lot next door,
her wonder brushed

impasto on words
you can't help but tongue:

Tyler Chadwick

Look. Rock. Roly-poly.
Reticular desires

relentless as the DNA
between us. As the verbs

we've fallen into. As
the pill bug carapace down

in her palm, parsing
the breeze, kicking air

to finally bring itself
right.

Field Notes on Language and Kinship

ENTRY 41

We do others violence when we fail to see their humanness then exert physical or emotional force to make them fit into our narrow vision of the world. During war this force is exerted on a massive scale by multiple parties who construct language to distance themselves from the destructive nature of their actions. In "I did not know, I only knew——" I address Jonathon Penny's "Confession, after Battle" (Fire 347) in which the speaker has broken down the distance between himself and his enemy and struggles with how to take up the demands other people's lives and deaths make on his language.

I did not know, I only knew—

At first glance, Jonathon Penny's "Confession, after Battle" seems a simplistic poem: the poet repeats the same structure for four, essentially five stanzas, changing only a word per stanzaic turn. The structure is thus something of a template—

> I'm sorry that I killed your _____
> I did not know he was your _____
> I only knew he was my enemy

—in which each blank is filled, respectively, with the words son, husband, father, brother. The rest of the language also seems simplistic, childish, perhaps, consisting of words many children learn—or could easily learn and use—early in their development.

But let's not confuse simple with simplistic, because Jonathon's poem is anything but simplistic. Sure, he essentially repeats the same stanza four, almost five times. But he does so with good reason: the speaker, obviously a soldier, is traumatized in the wake of a battle. The adrenaline has subsided. Perhaps he's looking over a field of fallen soldiers, considering the gratuitous destruction of war. Perhaps he's looked into the glassy eyes of his enemy and been struck by his humanness: *the man looks different now than he did through the scope of my rifle.* During this struggle, the soldier puts the man in context and sees him as part of a family—as a son, a husband and a lover, as a father, a brother. He, perhaps, enters the other man's life, recognizes himself in the Other.

And language fails him.

His thoughts become fragmentary, incomplete, as suggested by the lack of periods in the poem. The trauma of coming so suddenly and deeply into contact with an Other's humanness has disrupted his system of meaning, except that which matters most—and paradoxically, the least, because what signs and symbols can replace a human life?—in the moment: the language of grief, which flows so deeply in the subterranean river of human emotion as to be unspeakable.

So he prays. He confesses his grief to the soldier's mother, father, sister, brother, wife, son, daughter. He recites a litany, a ritualistic repetition meant to purge his sorrow, to bind him to the human community (as rituals are ultimately meant to do), to give him knowledge and meaning. Because in addition to grieving for the Other's life, he's also grieving over the annihilation of a system of meaning that taught him the Other was his enemy, that automatically placed the Other in opposition to the Self.

And that's how Jonathon leaves the poem: with his final line—"I did not know that he was not my enemy"—he exposes the devastating gaps (the naught, the emptiness) in the speaker's former epistemology. With that, he leaves it to readers to complete the final stanza, which seems to have been left intentionally unfinished—it's missing the third line ("I only knew he was my enemy") or a variation thereon just as it's missing the period. By so leaving the structure wide-open, he passes the torch to readers, offering no trite or easy conclusions, though I think a more filling and fulfilling epistemology is there, if only we look deeply enough to see.

THE GODS STEP OUT OF THEIR HIDING PLACE

PART 7: THE GODS STEP OUT OF THEIR HIDING PLACE

Joanna Brooks' poem "When the Mormons of Orange County Become Shin-toists" (*Fire* 68) asserts a progressive view of Mormonism. In this view, Latter-day Saints learn to fully live in and accept the material universe, which in terms of Mormon theology (as of Shinto beliefs) can't be separated from the spiritual universe. All spirit is matter, after all, as Joseph Smith taught. Hence: natural and constructed objects become places to develop or to sever our kinship with the spiritual realm. They channel focus either toward or away from eternal matters and relationships in the lives of those who meditate thereon. As such, these objects become shrines with which to honor or neglect the spiritual presence that infuses all things with light and life.

Mormonism holds that this presence includes our ancestors, the innumerable company of angels who assemble in and around our lives and who have a vested interest in our development. The greatest of this assembly is, of course, God, our Eternal Father, who possesses all things, a state of perfection some mistake for material success. Joanna represents this notion of perfection with "a gated community on a newly defaced hillside, each house with beige interiors, and a backyard oil drill banging its head against the clay like a mad grasshopper." Her language suggests that when humans reach for God via riches and worldly prestige, we ultimately remake the earth in our image, giving nature a second-rate facelift that neutralizes Earth's vibrancy and leaves scars the size of gated neighborhoods where one community cuts itself off from others. But this idea that the pursuit of perfection amounts to amassing wealth and prestige is madness, Joanna insists, that can only lead to banging the head against an earth meant for something else entirely.

Mormonism invites God out of this "hiding place" of an idea (to borrow Joanna's words) and brings the Maker down to Earth, revealing a once-mortal Being who, like all Gods before him, as Joseph Smith taught, learned how to be God "by going from a small capacity to a great capacity, from a small degree to another, from grace to grace, until the resurrection of the dead, from exaltation to exaltation," until he was "able to sit in everlasting burnings and everlasting power and glory as those who have gone before sit enthroned." This God is an accessible God, the fullness of whose glory is available to those who will honor and emulate him, who will see him as he is. This God is a social God inseparably connected with his Peers in Heaven (other exalted Beings) and his peers on Earth (his children, who have the potential to be exalted). This God thrills me beyond measure. His godhood speaks to me through the world, through my kinship with others, addressing my deepest yearnings. I pursue that voice through this section.

ENTRY 42

"For Rick" addresses an experience I had shortly after Jess and I moved our family from Ogden to Idaho Falls. Rick was a member of our local Mormon congregation—our ward— and I visited him one Sunday with two other men from the ward. He lived alone in a rented condo where he kept a room for four daughters who lived with his ex-wife and who only stayed with him every other weekend. From what I learned of the situation, Rick's divorce had been bitter, in large part because his wife had been unfaithful with a close family friend, whom she married shortly after the divorce was finalized. As we sat with Rick that day, I could tell he was still nursing his wounds.

He came to mind some months later when I first encountered J. Kirk Richards' 2004 painting Revelation. *Kirk's image shows a man raised off the ground, looking to heaven, his lower body wrapped in cloth that also flows around him like a question mark. His hands, feet, and side glow from within with Christ's stigmata. Reflecting on the image, I thought of Rick and began writing about our Sunday afternoon encounter. And I thought of "For Rick" a year or so later when I reread Marie Brian's poem "Spindrift" (Fire 64), especially the lines I've taken as my epigraph. As I interpret them, Rick's experience, Kirk's painting, and Marie's poem all take up the soul-defining encounter between faith and doubt.*

Field Notes on Language and Kinship

For Rick

the Undoubtable
Shot from your sea-swept eyes
—Marie Brian

On that Sunday afternoon we dropped in
on your first year divorced, slendered
into your secondhand couch like
three secondhand gods come to spare you

the gnawing of solitude. As you slid
a kitchen chair across berber the color
of prayer and sat alone in the bosom of the room,
soul mantled in memories stained amber with

oil, sweat, tears, we asked how you'd been.
Eyes deep as rosary beads blackened with use,
you looked up, told of your rib ripped from flesh,
of a twenty-year spouse spliced into the side

of your one-time friend, of four kids become
weekending guests to your solitude: the light stitches
God purled in your hope to keep the seams tight.
Fingers telling this knotted thread up your side

like Jacob climbing to God, you sidled up
to apocalypse and unraveled the hem of God's flame.
Before we left, you asked if we could pray, said
you'd speak as you softened your posture

instinctively pressed to the wound, then knelt,
gathered breath, blew open the curtains on God,
and, sifting his mystery, slid the sun from its arc,
quenched the bead in your brimful basin of soul,

and, balm aboil, clarified the room to a white stone
seared smooth in the smoldering palm of your words.

Tyler Chadwick   187

ENTRIES 43, 44, & 45

In "The Word that says everything—," "Your arms are open to something—," and "{ }" (which means null set) I take up different aspects of human creativity. The first entry responds to the creative power of language as I encountered it via Claire Åkebrand's poem "October Plush" (Fire 8). The second addresses art-making processes by reflecting on Sara Blaisdell's poem, "Ophelia" (Fire 62). In this entry, I speak specifically to the ways we produce and reproduce meaning via the creation and reception of art. And the third speaks to map-maker Jerry Gretzinger's obsessive world building. Since 1963 Gretzinger has been making and remaking and expanding a map of an imagined world, using a modified deck of cards to direct and randomize his creative process, which began as a doodle on a napkin and grew, 8x10 panel by 8x10 panel, to cover 1,600 square feet of surface area (as of 2012).

When I reread Glen Nelson's poem "Barbie Love" (Fire 299), a phrase from his penultimate line struck me as being relevant to the process I address in "{ }." Speaking to Barbie's emptiness and pliability as a toy and her potential to feed a child's fantasy (for good or for ill), Glen warns readers "to be careful" because Barbie's limbs gone errant could "poke out an eye." But what's more, if the doll's body gets manipulated in ways the material can't handle, "something inside the nothing snaps" and she comes undone.

Glen's language suggests that there's something obsessive about the relationship between a person and her/his fantasies. When someone pushes the limits of that relationship, manipulating—or trying to manipulate—material reality to match the fantasy, we often say they're artists or they're deluded (although the terms aren't necessarily mutually exclusive). For instance, when someone like Gretzinger wakes up day after day, decade after decade, and sets to work imposing his fantasy on the world by putting paint to paper, he becomes an artist, a maker. But when someone like Cho Seung-Hui (whose actions I explore in Entry 46) imposes on reality a world in which everyone conspires against him then he lashes out against that world, he becomes a mass murderer. "{ }" addresses the moments when something snaps in a person and s/he moves to fill that break via acts of making.

The Word that says everything—

Like the violet at its center, the texture of Claire Åkebrand's "October Plush" is lush, but only fleetingly so. The poet runs her words like fingers over the flower's petals, pausing in her passing by to notice the beauty of the transient subject at her feet. For although the violet can't get up and walk and although most species of violet are perennials—meaning the plant will be back next season—the flower is transient nonetheless: with the onset of autumn its petals "deflate" and it becomes increasingly "eager / for every last / hour of sun" because light is one of the only things that can extend its waning life. And as the earth tilts the flower's bed away from direct sunlight toward winter, the violet's reaching will ultimately be futile. It is, as Claire acknowledges, "dying."

But, as she also acknowledges by pressing the violet into her poem as someone might press a flower between the pages of a book, there is beauty in this transience. And melancholy as that beauty may be, it's still worth memorializing, if only because our words, we hope, will ward off death.

Looking into the eyes of our dead, standing and weeping over their bodies, holding their vesseled remains, watching their ashes circle to the earth—language rises to the tongue. We gather at viewings and funerals and wakes to sing and to pray, to embrace and to share memories, to clothe the spirit of grief in the language of kinship and praise. We write biographies, elegies, epitaphs, obituaries, sermons, odes. All in our attempts to address and to fill the absence left in our lives when someone or something we care about dies. Because, as Marcel Duchamp said, ironically enough on his own gravestone: "It's always other people who die." And maybe if we dress them in words as we dress them for burial the ironies of our shared mortality won't trail us to the grave.

Maybe our words will remain and grant us some measure of immortality.

Samuel Taylor Coleridge hoped as much. We have record of this hope in his short poem "Epitaph": "Stop, Christian passer-by!" he says, acknowledging the transient nature of mortality. "Stop, child of God, / And read [my epitaph] with gentle breast"—because, he seems to be saying, with each reading of this epitaph I "find life in death." My presence, housed in my words, passes to another generation. Yet, as they always will, in the presence of death words ultimately fail him. They can no more give us another life than they can ward off death. At most, perhaps, they can call forth and embody memories, which can in turn give us hope of reunion. But maybe language and memories and hope are enough to help us meet the gaze of death without giving way to despair.

Hence Claire's benediction to "October Plush." After parting ways with the curbside violet, which in the poem's world becomes an anthropomorphized representation of every "dying thing" the poet loves, she elevates her language to prayer in hopes of warding off the slow violence of entropy: "God Almighty," she says, "might this violence / not follow me into the shadows of my home, of winter." Despite this prayer, she certainly knows that death will follow her; but that's not the real irony at play here. The real irony arises out of the fact that, although Almighty God won't keep the violence of entropy from slowly wearing the poet's body and everything she loves to its proper end, he will eventually answer her prayer—and the many others like it that are prayed everyday—by speaking the words that will reverse the world's entropic flow and raise the poet and the poet's beloved to immortality. So even though the language we use in mortality is often ineffectual—including, of course, at making us immortal—the Divine Expression, the Word made flesh will, in the end, actually ward off death. And there's no language, no poetry—no *poesis*—more powerful than that.

Field Notes on Language and Kinship

Your arms are open to something—

Sara Blaisdell's "Ophelia" makes me a bit melancholy. As does the 1852 painting by John Everett Millais upon which I'm pretty sure it's based. As does Shakespeare's lady "of ladies most deject and wretched, / That suck'd the honey of [Hamlet's] music vows" and who, after falling in love with then being rejected by that "prick prince" (to use Sara's words), made her way into Shakespeare's brook, "dead men's fingers" wrapped around her neck; then into John Everett Millais' remix; then into Sara's purview and onto her wall (if the speaker in "Ophelia" can be trusted, anyway). It's uncanny, really, this layering of Ophelia's image: supporting dramatic character become subject of a Pre-Raphaelite obsession become mass-produced art print become lyric rumination on, among other things, art, the human condition, life after death—and the potential intersections thereof.

Speaking to the ways such reproductive layering widens the gap between the creation and reception of an artwork, Walter Benjamin—literary critic, philosopher, intellectual—wrote in 1936 that "that which withers in the age of mechanical reproduction is the aura of the work of art. This is a symptomatic process whose significance points beyond the realm of art" into broader cultural and natural landscapes, a process that speaks to the modern world's drifting away from contact with that which is authentic and original. Benjamin continues, "One might generalize by saying: the technique of reproduction detaches the reproduced object from the domain of tradition." In other words, the act of reproducing, say, a painting or even, to back a step further toward Creation itself, a panoramic landscape or a human body (as portrayed in a painting or a photograph or film), puts distance between the original and its audience. Such distancing, as Benjamin has it, diffuses the aura of the work, weakening its aesthetic impact, suppressing what aesthetic power and authority the original may bear by virtue of its having been touched and cared for by the creator and thus infused with something of the creator's life force.

But this life force doesn't exactly disappear. In fact, it may be that some of the original's aesthetic, cultural, and psychological DNA gets passed to each remixed, mass-produced, and mass-distributed copy spawned through the reproductive process. In this way, something of the parent work's genetics flow into and through its offspring, whose presence and countenance double for the aura of the parent and enter different cultures and traditions. Of course, they're not the parent's aura. But, to return to my point of departure, the doubling

Tyler Chadwick

effect inherent in the relationship among each displaced copy and between each copy and the original is uncanny—each repetition of or variation on the image may arouse in viewers a sense of familiarity with the image's aura: the copies look and feel a bit like the original. Yet, because the image has been decontextualized and re-purposed, it also becomes unfamiliar: although the copies may look and even in cases feel like the original artwork, they're not the original; they're copies. Any aura they bear is imitative and thus inauthentic.

But that doesn't make their aura or their influence any less real or affective. Consider, for instance, the case of Sara's "Ophelia": she has written a poem addressed to a character in a painting based on a character in a play. And while poem, painting, and play are each separated from the others by centuries, cultures, and artistic genres, the pathos they share is at once cumulative and re-iterative: poem comments on painting comments on play, which in turn adds aesthetic, cultural, emotional, and psychological value to the painting, which in turn adds aesthetic, cultural, emotional, and psychological value to the poem. And so on.

From the title, then, "Ophelia" comes drenched in associations: associations between the wry poet and the intended recipient of her cynicism, which bitterness may turn out to be, as the speaker claims, just a symptom of the poet's "jealous[y]." Associations between the poem and the crowded canon behind it: the mass-produced art print the poet purchased for "6.95 / at an art sale," the Millais painting the print imitates, the life and death of Shakespeare's supporting lady, even Christianity. Associations between this canon and the reader at least acquainted enough with Ophelia's tragic tale to catch the allusive pathos of the poem's subject and its potential to touch everyone, as the poet would have it, who has felt the pangs of life in a fallen world, of unreciprocated love. Who has death hanging over them like a cheap art print hung in "every room of the house." Who could find in that print—that lowly reproduction of Millais, which is really just a fictive reproduction of another fictive reproduction of flesh-and-blood humanity—a melancholy hope that even after death we "keep floating," we keep thinking, singing, reaching out for something (maybe what we, as Ophelia, "think [we] deserve": to be remembered) until we at last rise in the resurrection, which is ultimate proof that, like Ophelia, even though we may give up on ourselves and on each other, Christ never did and never will.

{ }

In mathematical sets, the null set, { }, also called the empty set, is the set that does not contain anything.

Obsession begins as a doodle scrawled
on a passing thought. Call it { }. Call it
the axiom nothing can satisfy. Call it
nothingness enfleshed: the void come to being
when fate intersects with desire and everything else
turns to naught. Call it decades of waking
to cartomancy and coffee, to minor arcana
and the infinite creep of impermanence.
Call it paracosmic immersion squared to
sprawling geography. Call it cartography
of the gods. Call the cartographer *Jerry*.
Watch him contour and crosshatch the incipient void
till it matches the shape of obsession,
till it sounds like a universe coming to birth.

ENTRY 46

As recorded in the King James Bible, the writer of Proverbs observed that "a wholesome tongue is a tree of life." Other versions of the text render "wholesome" as "gentle," "good," "healing," "peaceable," "soothing." While they each bring something different to the noun, these modifiers also collectively advocate for the productive use of the speech organ—for expressions that benefit the soul, that persuade self and others to moral goodness, that heal, that make peace, that console. In my segmented essay "The Tongue as Tree of Life: Meditations on Words and the Word and the Making of the World," I reflect on these uses of speech in terms of Mormon teachings about deity. As I wrote the essay, I was especially interested in exploring what influence these teachings have on the ways I think about how language functions in human communities—in other words, how language use can strengthen and/or destroy our relationships with others, with the earth, and with God.

I begin the essay by dropping my understanding of God into the stream of human language and experience and observing—then seeking to represent—how the ripples made by that understanding circle through and divert the stream. Hence the essay's format, in which I move associatively from meditation to meditation. Sometimes I let the ideas I address in one section flow directly into what ideas I address in the next and sometimes I circle back to or around something I've already said. But always: I try to keep the Gods' movements on the tip of my tongue, to somehow show with my words how the Makers might circle through and influence the eternities.

My epigraph for the essay comes from Casualene Meyer's "Why you should not bite your tongue (didactic poem #2)" (Fire 282), which speaks to the productive potential of human speech. And I conclude the essay by applying the ideas I address in my meditations in a reading of Gideon Burton's sonnet "Salt and Blood" (Fire 74).

The Tongue as Tree of Life: Meditations on Words and the Word and the Making of the World

It comes to this:
angels will to dance on the tip of your tongue
and your own words want to bounce just once
then dive into others without waves.
—Casualene Meyer

1.

Laying on a toddler bed one night with my almost two-year-old daughter, waiting for her breathing to slow and her body to relax against sleep, I stared at the brightly-illustrated solar system projected onto the ceiling by a novelty night-light. The image's yellows and oranges had begun to fade, leaving the planets just outlines against a blue backdrop. The coloring book image—the blueprint—that remained, half-filled-in and fading, called to mind what I understood of the Gods' creative process. As Moses wrote, the Gods divided light from darkness, then the waters from earth; then came vegetation; then fishes, whales, and fowl; then beasts and creeping things; then humans, the Cosmos-Makers' race. This wasn't a one shot deal, though, taken on pell-mell. Before they could start building, the Makers needed a plan. They needed to set the process in order. So, standing before the Void, they watched the universe unfold in their minds before they ever took in hand the materials they would need to construct it.

2.

Scratch that.

I said the Makers took the components of the universe *in hand* as they built it, but that doesn't feel quite right. I'll try that sentence again: The Gods watched the universe unfold in their minds before they ever took on the tongue the materials they would need to construct it. By *took on the tongue* I don't of course mean that, like small children or animals, the Gods actually took objects to mouth. No, I mean that after they had formed things in the mind they formed them with the tongue, speaking things into being, persuading them into existence. Hence John: In the beginning was the Word, the *Logos*, the Revelation of God, the Divine Interjection, the Makers' Tongue.

3.

Before I go on: It occurs to me that, speaking as a Latter-day Saint, I may have taken some things for granted here based on my reading of Mormon teachings about Deity:

First, that the Gods are Makers: they create and they procreate.

Second, the Makers' plurality: I assume not a singular Entity acting as lone Creator but a coterie of creative Beings acting in concert, a Community of Gods.

Third, that the Makers are a Community of female and male Beings: I assume gendered Makers who reside in socialities similar to those we form here, Eternal Beings equally coupled within an eternal marriage covenant who complement each other in their creative and procreative work.

Fourth, the plurality of the Makers' creations: I assume these Beings have created and peopled not just this world, this universe, but many worlds and many universes.

Fifth, that Creation doesn't occur *ex nihilo*: I assume the Makers build things from materials extant in expansive cosmos.

Sixth, that Creation unfolds in an eternal round: I assume that the Makers' creative acts occur in the present progressive tense, that these Beings haven't just created, they are creating.

Seventh, that humans are the Makers' offspring: I assume that we have the making gene in us and that by virtue of heredity and training, we can emulate our Parents and become Makers ourselves.

Eighth, that the Makers have bodies of flesh and bone: else how procreate? Else how interact with objects and materials? Else how, without form, form things with the tongue?

4.

A thing, at its root, is an assembly, a deed, an event, a material object, a body, a being. To tongue some thing, then, is to assemble, to act, to make happen, to embody, to be, to become with the organ of speech.

5.

As soon as my youngest daughter could stand and walk, she liked to perform for the family from my in-laws' hearth: standing where she had seen her older sisters stand to stage their impromptu recitals—where her mother and aunts and uncle also stood as kids—she made sounds, babbling like children do in the

Field Notes on Language and Kinship

phase just before language. I say *before*, but, really, this sounding is part of the language making process. Having heard the spoken word since her ear bones developed during gestation, she instinctively learned to create the stream she heard coming from others' mouths, babbling as if she were making words. As she developed from an infant into a toddler, she began plucking words like pebbles from the stream and, as infants and toddlers do when they handle new objects, playing with them in her mouth until her mind and her tongue learned the poses needed to intelligibly articulate those words, until she learned to connect the tactile sensation of assembling a word on the tongue with the object or objects that sensation represents.

As she made more connections—her first was among the word "Mom" and her mother *and* me; in fact, she often called me "Mom" in the months after she started talking—I noticed the pleasure she took both in connecting lingual sensations with objects and in knowing she had been understood by others, in knowing she had brought us pleasure through her language making. The day she first married "bird" with the robins and starlings that frequented our backyard, she stood at the back window and pointed at each animal, repeating "Buhrt! Buhrt! Buhrt!" with the urgency and excitement of a breakthrough. And it was a breakthrough: she was making language, which we celebrated with clapping and smiles and phone calls to grandparents and which her sisters celebrated for months (though less frequently as her vocabulary grew) by asking her, "Where are the birds?" and watching her run to the window where she asked, "Buhrt? Buhrt?" and looked and pointed and waited for the robins and starlings to return.

6.

While I was running one summer morning along Ogden's east bench, twenty or so yards in front of me a single dove landed in the middle of the road, followed shortly thereafter by a companion. Reluctant to break the rhythm of my run, I kept going. But twenty yards further down the street from where the birds had landed, I gave in to serendipity, to the potential symbolism of the moment, and turned back to watch the birds, to record the occurrence by taking some pictures with my phone.

As the doves crossed lanes, making for a nearby driveway, a Jeep passed. Its engine was heavy even against my ears and I thought it would startle the birds to flight, but they continued undisturbed. Their contentment called me after them and I followed to the driveway, lagging behind and watching from a distance as they stopped to pick at a pile of bird seed that had been spilled near the lawn's edge. Squatting on the sidewalk easement six or so feet from the feeding birds, I looked on and took some pictures as they each stooped to gather seed then stood to regard me, then stooped again.

At one point, the dove farthest from me skirted behind its companion and resumed its feeding ritual from the edge of the spill nearest me. I'm not sure what prompted the move—the prodding of Providence, curiosity, instinct, a change in the breeze, access to more desirable seed, etc. Neither am I certain what significance to assign our brief encounter nor even that it need be assigned great significance. Isn't it enough, I ask myself, to have crossed paths with these doves, to have been allowed by what seemed their obvious socialization with humans to regard them—and to be regarded by them—from a distance that may have threatened other, more skittish birds? Wasn't it enough to have been present with them for a while, to hold them in my mind as they may have held me in theirs?

7.
Some things exist in the space beyond words. For instance:

My morning encounter with the doves.

The physical sensation of moving across the earth, lungs burning in warm summer air, muscles in the acid produced by exertion.

The lingual sensation of tonguing words, the pleasures of assembling speech.

Listening to a child's breathing get heavy as her body slips beneath cover of sleep.

The coming together and the erasure of bodies.

8.
The morning of April 16, 2007, Cho Seung-Hui, a 23-year-old college student, killed 33 people (himself included) and injured 17 others in a spree shooting on the campus of Virginia Tech University. Brooding over the day's chaos, over the emptiness of Cho's spectacle, the void his performance ripped open in the world, poet Bob Hicok responded by making language. Hicok teaches at Virginia Tech and had been in close contact with many who were affected by the tragedy, including Cho, whom Hicok once had as a student; so as a poet—from the Greek *poietes*, meaning "maker"—Hicok seems especially invested in assembling language events that might help him and others begin remaking lives rent by loss.

In a series of poems published in his 2010 collection, *Words for Empty and Words for Full*, he takes up this process, circling around the massacre, trying to make sense of his role in the tragedy and its aftermath.

But is *aftermath*, Hicok asks in his poem "Whimper," the right name to give something that "never ends"? The word originally referred to a second crop of grass grown after the first had been mown or harvested, so it connotes the attempt to begin anew following a destructive event. But what if the devastation continues once the initial burst of violence has passed? What if for victims of violence there ultimately is no "after," no cue that turmoil has ended and stability returned? What if the insistence of erasure forestalls *any* effort to address violence and loss and to rebuild?

For example: while trying to compose this and the next section of my essay, I brooded over Cho's multimedia manifesto. Circling around the assemblage of video, images, and text that surfaced shortly after the massacre, I hoped to parse his motivations, to discover some logic behind his unspeakable acts— as if ascribing his performance a sense of logic would help me directly address its effects in light of the Mormon doctrine of makers and making. However, his manifesto isn't quite manifest: the incoherence of his language eludes the fullness of exchange. Put simply: his declaration doesn't really say anything; and because it essentially says nothing, when I engaged his words I was drawn into their void. Even though I wasn't directly affected by the massacre, even though no one I knew was erased by Cho's erasure, my language became slippery in its presence. My words refused to settle on a coherent narrative. I felt for a time as if had been ravished by Cho's tongue.

9.

In his profanity-thick diatribe, Cho addresses an unnamed "you," pointing, or rather raising the middle finger at someone else, no, *anyone* else for making him do what he "had to." By which he seems to have meant that others' actions and attitudes forced him to, in his words, begin cleaning America's slate of Satan's Descendants, "Apostles of Sin," "Lovers of Terrorism," "Hedonists, Charlatans, Sadists, Rapists"—and Virginia Tech, he for some reason believed, was as good a place as any to begin cleaning. The video recording, which presents Cho reading excerpts from his manifesto as well as speaking extemporaneously about his motivations, shows him at times weary, as if he were speaking from the edges of sleep, and at times irate, declaiming his credo like a Modernist poet-seer delivering dire prognostications for the human race: his lips pursed, his voice intense, a somber drone, the tone generally rising at caesuras and sentence breaks as if at once to question each statement as it's made and to interrogate his intended audience. At various points his interrogatives come in litanies of questions or phrases, as with the following:

> You had everything you wanted. Your Mercedes wasn't enough, you brats? Your golden necklaces weren't enough, you snobs? Your trust fund wasn't enough? Your vodka and cognac weren't enough? All your debaucheries weren't enough? Those weren't enough to fulfill your hedonistic needs? You had everything.

Cho, on the other hand, felt that he had nothing. Even the things he may have had to at least make his manifesto productive—his questions—seemed to take him nowhere and to do nothing because they were directed at anyone and thus at no one. This is underscored by the fact that, as Hicok suggests in his poem "In the Loop," for whatever reason—be it because Cho was bullied, depressed, overwhelmed with self-doubt, or otherwise abused and unstable, we may never know why for sure—the boy "felt / that he was nothing." And because he believed that *some thing* (his being in the world) could be *no thing*—a belief that is at its root a destructive metaphor—he attempted to make his peers equal to him by taking every thing they had by first taking their lives. Then, intending to become a martyr for his gospel, he gave in to his metaphor, entering its attempt to erase Being by killing himself.

Yielding to the destructive potential of an unsound metaphor, in life as in death Cho erased and was erased. In the process he ultimately "unworded" himself, as Hicok puts it in a poem titled "So I Know." To be unworded is to be unsaid, unexpressed, unuttered, unspoken, unspeakable, without words, without description, stripped of language, stripped of speech. Hicok suggests that Cho was all of these (though in not so many words), that the boy wore silence like a mask—or as the poet says in "Mute," like "a shadow under the awning of his cap," a shroud that obscured how others understood him. Hicok takes responsibility for the way he personally read Cho's muteness: Because Cho had "lived tongueless" in his teacher's presence, Hicok hadn't felt the boy "was human," which of course implies that the teacher saw his untongued student as something other-than-human. After all, to be human is to have language, which we metonymically describe as having a tongue.

Hicok admits to not being the only one who saw otherness in Cho's si-

Field Notes on Language and Kinship

lence: When the boy's manifesto surfaced, Hicok says those "who knew him" felt "it was nearly / an out-of-body experience / to hear him speak." Many who remember Cho remember him as a social misfit whose coarse silence caused friction in his relationships. Some of his former high school classmates even mention how he often ignored others' attempts to strike up conversation with him. So the chance to hear Cho speak, even from beyond the grave, may have allowed those who knew him but hadn't ever heard him to finally get a sense of his humanness. His postmortem voice can't fill his erasure, though; instead, the perpetual unfolding of his performance beyond the initial event perpetuates what Hicok calls "a speech of null / and void." Hicok notes that such language "actively draw[s] in the nothing" that more social others "long to occupy / with song and chatter," the "vacancy" among bodies that many humans "seek to fill" with meaningful sounds to the end of meaningful exchange. Cho, it seems, desired and perpetrated this void. He "let it fill him, let nothing" ravish his lexicon until his final means of expression was erasure, until his last recourse was to be unmade, until his tongue twisted into the question mark that still punctuates—that may always punctuate—the erasure made by his massacre.

10.

To twist the tongue is to question, to test, the body's organ of speech.
> Peter Piper picked a peck of pickled peppers.
> She sells sea shells by the sea shore.
> The sixth sick sheik's sixth sheep's sick.

Twist too violently, though, and the tongue comes undone.

11.

The evening of December 14, 2012, while driving with my family through a snow storm to a Christmas dinner at our church building, I listened to my six-year-old daughter explain the water cycle. "I know how water works," she said. "It goes from the ground to the sky and gets fluffy and turns into a cloud and then the cloud gets big and drops the water to Earth and it starts all over again and it's called the water cycle." As I heard her relate what she had learned in school that day and considered how the water cycle sustains and renews the earth, I nearly wept, as I had earlier that day, for the community of Newtown, Connecticut. Instead, I prayed for my daughters and their futures and for Newtown because I thought the community would desperately need divine sustaining and renewal after Adam Lanza stormed Sandy Hook Elementary, took 27 lives (including his own), and in the process thrust the community's kids into a tragedy mine could hardly comprehend—scratch that: into a tragedy hardly anyone—if anyone—could comprehend. Being itself balks at such violence, weeping from wounds before the ruptured tissue heals or life yields to death. Whatever the case, though, whether the end of violence is healed wounds or death, an erasure remains that both demands to be addressed and that resists our attempts to address it.

But still some of us try.

The day of the Sandy Hook shooting, *The Onion*, satirical online news rag, ran an article titled "F—— Everything, Nation Reports." The article is short—it comes in at only 456 words—but as the title suggests, its language is potent: of the many profanities included, 16 are the f-word. It begins: "Following the fatal shooting this morning at a Connecticut elementary school that left at least 27 dead, including 20 small children, sources across the nation shook their heads, stifled a sob in their voices, and reported f—— everything. Just f—— it all to hell." Besides representing the shock, horror, and hopelessness many Americans experienced that winter day, the article's use of profanity—the f-word, especially—suggests that humans often turn to forceful language when confronted with things we're otherwise unable to address: the pain of stubbing a toe or slicing a finger or smashing a thumb with a hammer. Frustration at not getting our way or not having been heard (this seems to have been one reason for Cho's profanity-laden manifesto). The terror of staring into a void ripped open in the world through violent events and not knowing how to respond to the erasure.

Because such things are often unspeakable, as a result we may try to impose our will on them with more forceful uses of the tongue. Consider, for instance, how the f-word functions: at its root, the verb means to copulate with, to thrust, to strike, to push. In line with its meaning, the word's verbal expression is forceful: a fricative followed by a half-open central vowel closed abruptly—violently, even—with an obstruent. This means of expression, when combined with the word's definition, makes the term an easy representation of a speaker's perceived potency, of the way s/he understands the ability to influence things with the tongue.

But just to say "f—— everything" won't work if we, as makers, intend to counteract being's erasure with our acts of verbal intercourse. That work of renewal requires subtler, more productive acts of lingual power and influence.

Field Notes on Language and Kinship

12.

Hence: poetry, from the Greek *poesis*, meaning the process of making.

13.

To tongue poetry is to make some thing with the organ of speech. A new world, perhaps. Maybe lasting peace. At the very least, a language event that might help us remake lives rent by violence and loss.

14.

Take, for instance, the following:

I like the taste of Gideon Burton's "Salt and Blood" (*Fire* 74). No, I don't live in a coven or avoid sunlight and, although I do like potato chips, NaCl isn't really my thing. Nonetheless, Gideon's sonnet "Salt and Blood" makes my lyric tastebuds tingle. Read it aloud. Hear the lines densely-packed with sounds that spring off the tongue, as here, "that burning morning bursting hot-white call / of crimson dazzling awe." And here, "yet He lets that peace in pieces shatter, / and what had glowed a grace-fierce fire, sputter." Hear the lines densely-packed with sounds that spring off the tongue. Let the open vowels in the first four lines especially crack open the jaw and the palate: the "aw" of each *-all* word and their "hot" counterpart, the long *a*'s in "grey drape," the short *a* of "dampen" and "dazzling," the straggling, not quite assonant *o*'s in "morning" and "world." Savor the alliterative interplay between the *l*'s, *m*'s, *d*'s, *b*'s, *h*'s, *t*'s, *c*'s, *w*'s, and the sibilance of the *s*'s.

All this sound and tongue work in the octet creates a bit of friction that immediately gets cooled by the sestet's opening line, which slows the poem's speed to a more meditative pace: "Cold desert, colder night, stark sky a stone." The phonetic combo *ol* (which also comes in line eight) further opens the palate and sets the meditative tone and pace of the sestet because the *l* seems to extend the *o*, a lengthening that carries over into "stone." As I read it, the cumulative effect of these sounds and this move to a more meditative posture creates "[a] thirst inside a hunger," a desire to be filled and healed that can only be satisfied as we slow down the speed of modern living, including the speed with which we make language, which sometimes gets translated into breakneck prayers, into prayers spoken on-the-go.

Now, mobile prayer is well and good and encouraged in scripture as the directive to "pray always." But we really shouldn't let it make up our entire repertoire of communication with God. We still need to fall, in each sense of that term: we needed to fall from God's presence, as did Adam and Eve, in order 1) to struggle alone in and to face the erasures of the lone and dreary world so we could develop our agency and independence and 2) to be reminded that, ultimately, the communion and the communication of grace is our only means of returning home—we have to learn to rely on each other. And to experience redemptive expressions of grace, we need to fall before our Maker, to slow down and approach him, to worship him with desire made efficacious on the tongue. The closing lines of "Salt and Blood" enact and encourage such slowing down with the repeated preposition in the list, which makes the mouth—and hopefully the mind—linger a bit longer on each item: "to shake, to scrape, to kneel and stutter-speak; / to taste the salt and blood of Him I seek."

This final line not only points up our physical, mental, and spiritual experience of Christ's sacrifice, wherein he sweat great drops of blood as he absorbed the violence of the Fall and in process extended his grace across the erasures of human experience. It also points up the rhetorical effects of Gideon's poem, which speaks to the cycle of redemption—the world's perpetual re-making—even as it encourages readers' participation in that cycle through the lingual acts it inspires. "Salt and Blood," then, is a redemptive event, a lyric offering of peace and grace, an expression of the Makers' Tongue.

And its palate tastes oh so good.

ENTRIES 47 & 48

Both "Upon learning, at thirty-one, that my astrological sign had been changed from Sagittarius to Ophiuchus—"and "Upon hearing Elder B—— bear witness that 'Satan is real' to a Mormon congregation the second Sunday of 2011—"converse with Elizabeth Garcia's poem "God as Intern" (Fire 184–85). The God I depict in "Upon learning" is a direct response to the apprentice-God of Liz's poem, while my portrayal of the father and sons in "Upon hearing" plays further with the idea of how gods-in-training might develop or not into godhood.

Upon learning, at thirty-one, that my astrological sign had been changed from Sagittarius to Ophiuchus—

I split my tongue taste-testing the serpent bearer's anapest, clave desire
tongue-tracing the equinoctial groove: linea negra long as the tracks on
God's favorite L.P.: the adagios he composed and recorded while an intern
in his dad's studio, the ones he still plays as he paints, flings timbral aeons
to the infinite corners of his canvas as he dances at the infinite edge—
a slow breaking two-step, his body long and low in divination's groove,
flesh folded into movement folded into universe folded into the technique
he picked up from Pollock when the artist came upstate for a show
and gifted the Creator his latest meditation, its fractals spinning out and out
till they shed the ground like so much paint and God knit them into skin
to clothe this uncertainty of a universe, to graft into the stories I recite
as I wait to shed this skin and slip into the serpent's sidereal maw.

Upon Hearing Elder B——— Bear Witness that "Satan is Real" to a Mormon Congregation the Second Sunday of 2011—

I watched my almost-three-year-old pick lint from her hand-me-down pink
                                                                        tights,
considered how quickly they'd unravel if she kept teasing that stray mid-thigh
                                                                        string—
obsessing it loose from the nylon weave—and whether the thread would
                                                                        stretch
from our pew to God's, though I imagined that empty, imagined him out fish-
                                                                        ing the Snake,
waves lapping at his waders like a dog left alone all day whose humans have
                                                                        homed heavy
with the scent of attention, the scent of desire insatiate as the current run par-
                                                                        allel God's lures:
the Hal Smith and Black Magnum Leech he tied for his boys before their Hells
                                                                        Canyon run
an aeon ago, the winter his second went serial, slit his upbringing anus to jaw
like the limit of steelhead they took that trip: gore, shit, scales, and the perfect
                                                                        planes
of omega-rich meat chafing his pathology grown obsessive as his knife's even
                                                                        slice
anus to jaw—and repeat—and repeat—and again—his pathology grown
                                                                        vulpine
as the legion that whispered with the gore from his brother's side when the
                                                                        impatient blade
thought the crucifix too slow and slipped in to finish before Father could un-
                                                                        ravel the temple veil
to get line enough to suture the grave, to finish the Olive Matuka he was tying
when the sheriff showed, said Lucifer's M.O. had surfaced downstream Eden:
                                                                        fig split ostiole
to stalk and snagged in the back-whorl where undercut bank exposed tree
                                                                        roots like fish ribs
scavenged free flesh by the gulls whose hunger has stalked God to impotence
                                                                        since he
shooed them with buckshot from Eden's bowels and sent cherubim to cover
                                                                        the corpse

Field Notes on Language and Kinship

until his firstborn could perfect his cast enough to finesse new flesh from the

Styx.

ENTRY 49

In "On Crucifixion *by J. Kirk Richards" I ask after secrets only a god would know. I do this through a meditation on Kirk's imposing image of Christ at the moment of death (painted in 2004). Two lines from Steven L. Peck's poem "Winter Gifts" (Fire 339) speak directly to my asking. Wondering why "the dark-eyed juncos" stick around during winter when the world is bleak and the food sources scarce, Steve concludes that "The calculus of their presence brokers / a secret only a god would know."* "On Crucifixion" *takes up the calculus of Christ's presence in the world and the mystery of how and why that presence influences the universe.*

On *Crucifixion* by J. Kirk Richards

Some seduction, this—flesh stripped of sweat,
blood, breath, soul; his body gone limp at the crux
of God's mystery, shipped home C.O.D.
in a crate stamped "Fragile," and pinned
to the threshold of paradox like a sack spit
by vespers into the neighbor's vining buds.
From here, leaf chatter and whisper of plastic
sound like questions shedding their skin:
When God cross-dresses in death, does
the universe blush? Does it worship
the crimson-stained grain of his skin,
the shadow of his ribs? Does it praise
his left breast until milk warms the tongue
like redemption? Like silence? Like blasphemy?

ENTRIES 50 & 51

"Is There Deep Play in Heaven?" and "This neighborhood, too, has its underbelly—" address the notion of Mormon piety through my responses to Paul Swenson's poem "Negative Space" and Laura Nielson Baxter's poem "Take Care of Your Soul—It's Flapping in the Breeze" (Fire 29). (Paul's contribution to Fire in the Pasture is on pages 406–12 of the anthology.) In both responses, I explore how LDS ideas of morality and righteousness, as perpetuated via Mormon cultural beliefs and practices, can keep Mormons from experiencing the deep beauties of Mormon theology and can harm those with whom Mormons interact who don't make the effort to look beyond the appearance of Mormon piety.

The title of the second entry is a line from Elisa Pulido's "Dog Walking at Night in a New Neighborhood" (Fire 363–64) in which the poem's speaker considers what might be happening beneath the tidy appearance of her environment.

Is There Deep Play in Heaven?

> *On the afternoon of the first*
> *resurrection, I want to sit on my sister May's bench and read*
> *her new poems. So, maybe, if you're still around when I go under,*
> *I wonder—could you burn me, turn me into ash, and slip me in*
> *[the family plot] somewhere?*
> —Paul Swenson

I received news the morning of Friday, February 3, 2012, from Paul Swenson's good friend and fellow poet Alex Caldiero that Paul had passed away around noon the previous Thursday. I didn't know Paul personally but I do know for certain that his passing, which came after a long bout of unsettled health, leaves a void in the world of Mormon poetry, one that may continually be filled with the language he left behind and with any language and personal and cultural change that language inspires.

Paul had a playful, Blues-inspired lyric and his poems often come across as clever and witty—even, to some, bitter—more than profound. In fact, Deseret News' Jerry Johnston panned *Iced at the Ward, Burned at the Stake,* Paul's first poetry collection and an exploration of (among other things) Mormon conceptions of deity, ritual, and embodiment, as a "waste [of] space," the overly playful ravings of a Scrooge. (Odd image that: raising a playful Ebenezer. . .) Stephen Carter suggests that while the "interpretation of Mormonism" Paul explores in his poems is, yes, "forever inventive, forever reflective, and forever playful," Paul's playfulness is "deep." It's more than mere wit, more than a child's attempt to inflame his elders, as Johnston suggests it is. Stephen observes that Paul's "deep play" works after the manner theorized by Jeremy Bentham, British utilitarian philosopher, though Bentham was curmudgeonly about the benefits of such play. Says Stephen, Bentham "describes deep play as when a person is engaged in an activity where, 'the stakes are so high that . . . it is irrational for anyone to engage in it at all, since the marginal utility of what you stand to win is grossly outweighed by the disutility of what you stand to lose.'" As Jennifer Reifsneider, Curator of Collections at the Missoula Art Museum, has it in her discussion of the "joyful revelry and subversive whimsy" present in the MAM collection, deep play "arises when the potential for loss far outweighs the potential for gain." So it occurs when the player gambles social, cultural, and spiritual standing against a compulsion to play with subjects others think too serious to consider with anything less than deep solemnity (if at all)—as when a Mormon poet tinkers publicly with religious and cultural taboos (like Mother in Heaven and sexuality), exposing himself, as it were, on the chapel's front lawn. (In reference to this, I think of the cover image on *Iced at the Ward, Burned at the Stake*, in which Paul is pictured outside an LDS chapel, singing at a candlelight vigil for one of his friends during her church court.)

But isn't a poet in part someone who instinctively plays with words, and who plays with them deeply and well? Someone who, in process of such playing, speaks to our deepest personal and cultural needs and desires? Poetry is a mark of cultural health, an indication, as Pulitzer Prize winning poet Robert Hass says, that "a lot of people [in the culture are] literate and alive." This is so because "[y]ou have to have some kind of interior life to make" and to enjoy "a work of art and in a world as busy and heedless as this one we need all the consciousness we can muster" in order not to wither on the vine, as it were. So poetry—like living a creative life, in general—comes in part of introspection and carries with it an abiding awareness that the inner life matters. And it matters not only because deepening our awareness of what's on the inside requires that we make time to ponder, to sift through and reflect upon matters of the soul and our lived experience in the world. But also because self-awareness and creativity require imagination, which enables us to step into another's soul and to consider the world as experienced from another's perspective. Because imagination ultimately isn't confined to the boundaries of lived experience, it becomes space of endless, deep play—space where the conscious and less-than-conscious minds come together to question, to make sense of, to critique, and to expand our relationship with the material and immaterial worlds.

Paul, like his sister, May Swenson, before him, occupied and pushed against the boundaries of this space. Sometimes these siblings even tried to represent the space concretely on the page. May did it more extensively than Paul, but Paul tried it, nonetheless. In her concrete poem, "Bleeding," May lets space trickle through the text, as in this excerpt:

> Stop bleeding   said the knife
> I would if I   could said the cut.
> Stop bleeding   you make me messy with the blood.
> I'm sorry   said the cut.
> Stop or   I will sink in farther said the knife.

Field Notes on Language and Kinship

In conjunction with the poem's content, I view this gap as a representation of trickling blood, a gaping wound, the gap between women (the seeping gash) and men (the unrelenting knife). This negative space thus contributes to the meaning of the poem.

Paul did something similar with his aptly titled poem, "Negative Space," in which he talks, of all things, about the difficulty of "being Mormon / and having"—*gasp*—"nipples." The text of the poem is presented in two pointed columns. The left column opens to the right, like a "less-than" sign; and the right opens to the left, like "greater than." Taken together these columns circumscribe a diamond-shaped inner court. Negative space is thus quite literally at the center of Paul's poem. And this emptiness signifies the negative space present a) in the poet's life as a joyfully embodied being, one who took pleasure in "[h]aving hard nipples," in being fully sexed and fully sexual even though he lived amidst a people often conditioned to be suspicious of and to put off the body and its needs and desires; and b) in the mind of Mormon culture generally, where the Church correlated body—as the mannequins and comic strip bodies in the poem—has been stripped of its nipples. This "censor[ed]," "emasculated," "nervously neutered" male body is meant to be the standard against which everyday Mormons—including Mormon women—gauge their sexuality. But, the poet points out, this body is "purely negative space." Its presence, he seems to be saying, represents the conspicuous absence of erotic desire, of sexual play—even of cultural play—in much of Mormonism's religious and cultural aesthetic.

So Paul, the poet, frolicked in this space, filling it with Blues-infused rhythms, with everyday language and passions and conviction, with earthly meditations on the divine. By so singing the body electric, I think he hoped to stir the kingdom up a bit, to encourage his readers to think a bit more deeply about and to play a bit more deeply with the popular, though perhaps not fully doctrinal, beliefs and institutions of Mormonism. And all this to the end of facilitating a more expansive "Mormon mind" and soul. This expanded being is one that could eventually be assigned, perhaps, to organize "the big reunion party," as Paul calls the celestial afterlife in his poem "Family Plot"—or could we call it an after party? Here Paul and his sister—and anyone else who would care to join them—gather in an open field the afternoon of the first resurrection, sharing new and old poems, playing deeply, wittily, imaginatively, with the structure of the universe, with Heaven's language, Heaven's culture, and Heaven's institutions. Their incorruptible bodies fully nippled, eternally rested, eternally ripe.

This neighborhood, too, has its underbelly—

Laura Baxter's poem, "Take Care of Your Soul—It's Flapping in the Breeze," is an exercise in absurdity. I mean, a neighbor airing his soul on a clothesline like recently washed laundry then leaving it to dry for a few decades? How absurd! But this premise hasn't been pushed to absurdity just for absurdity's sake. This is poetry, after all, the realm of metaphor, metonymy, synecdoche, hyperbole— a place where language (itself a realm of metaphor, metonymy, synecdoche) is pushed to its limits. A place where one image, concept, or any part thereof stands in for another image, concept, or part thereof. A place of deep play, where not everything should be taken at face value.

As in the realm of piety, where not every display of righteousness should be taken at face value. Consider the Pharisees, for instance, those make-sure-others-see-me-praying-on-the-street-corner saints whom Christ chided with a striking simile: "Woe unto you, scribes and Pharisees, hypocrites! for ye are like unto whited sepulchres, which indeed appear beautiful outward, but are within full of dead men's bones, and of all uncleanness." In "Take Care," Laura tweaks and updates this comparison, making it less macabre, more suburban Utah (her home and the setting of many of her poems), where overt displays of Mormon piety can border on the Pharasaic and are often rewarded in the Latter-day Saint social structure wherein the degree of one's faith is often judged in acts of service performed, motivations and actual righteousness notwithstanding. I think, for example, of a former Church leader I knew who was so busy serving and gaining social status and praise in the Church and his local community that he neglected his wife and kids to the point where his wife finally asked for a divorce. Or another well-loved leader who cheated on his wife with a married woman he was counseling. Or a father who sexually abused his step-daughter, all the while "honoring" his position in the Church. Or apparently-devoted, marriage-covenant-honoring husbands whose late-night pornography addictions and untempered lust turn into covert flirtations—and beyond—with co-workers.

While such uncleanness may be the exception and the extremity in a religion that preaches the sanctity of familial bonds and among a people who strive to practice and to embody that sanctity in their daily lives because, as we're fond of repeating, "no other success can compensate for failure in the home," such hypocrisies are also, to put it simply, dangerous. Laura observes the danger embodied in such acts of hypocrisy—and so moves to air Mormonism's cultural laundry—when she says her neighbor's "hung" "soul" is "like a warning sign: / 'Beware of Dog' / but slightly more dangerous because souls are involved." And not just the "abandoned soul" of this "[v]icious," "crafty and elusive man" whose sins we don't know, save his hypocrisy, which, paradoxically with his piety, is couched in metaphor and on public display day after day, year after year, decade after decade. But also the souls of those who fail to see and are taken in by his pretension and lack of integrity. To see him as he is, then, is to see him "Un-souled." And in the Mormon cosmology, which posits that the spirit and the body constitute the soul and that the soul is redeemed through Christ's atonement, this suggests that the poet's pious neighbor has denied himself the physical and spiritual redemption offered in mortality and beyond only in an abiding relationship with and through emulation of Christ. Because of this denial, the neighbor is ultimately not at one with God, with his neighbors, with himself.

Maybe, then, as the poem's final stanza suggests, someone should remind him (and the culture that has enabled his hypocrisy) that he's "forgotten" something—"the weightier matters of the law," perhaps: judgment, mercy, faith—and that in so doing he's hung himself out to dry. By virtue of his denial of the atonement, he has crucified Christ afresh. Any maybe, just maybe, his poet-neighbor—this player with words—is someone who can do the reminding.

On the other hand, the poet's insistent neighbor-watching might be just another manifestation of piety. So maybe, it's best that she keep her comments to herself.

Tyler Chadwick

When I first read Sunni Brown Wilkinson's poem "Acrobats" (Fire 476) her story felt familiar: she's approached on the street by a transient who asks a question she hesitates to answer and the encounter sticks with her (else why reflect on it in a poem?). A short time before reading "Acrobats" I had experienced something similar on a morning run. I've reflected on that encounter in a poem, "For the Man in the Red Jacket" (Fire 105), and in a short essay about Grandpa Chadwick, "His word more than his face remains—." Both poem and essay address, as my meditation on "Acrobats" addresses, the concepts of mercy and grace.

The title of my response to Sunni's poem, "The pull of human mercy—," is a phrase from Laura Hamblin's poem "To Baptize" (Fire 201). "To Baptize" critiques the Mormon practice of baptizing children once they've turned eight. Laura says in her poem that this is unnecessary for her son, who in her mind doesn't need to be saved "from being human" by other humans who, after all, could only pull him from baptismal waters with "the pull of human mercy"—and that isn't on par with the pull of divine mercy. Whereas Laura's use of the phrase suggests that human mercy may be cut off from the divine, my use of the phrase implies that the small mercies we extend to others contain traces of and can develop into a fullness of mercy and grace.

The pull of human mercy—

Sunni Brown Wilkinson's "Acrobats" explores rhetorics of grace. It contrasts the simple and scripted made-for-TV "piety"—an easily imitated and consumed brand commodified and encouraged by the (early morning? early afternoon?) televangelist—with the speaker's own halting attempts to "awaken [her] faith" to something beyond play-acting, beyond miming the preacher "in front of the mirror." The pathos of her attempt—the depth of its influence on her, faltering as the attempt seems to be—is evident in the imagery she uses to describe "the homeless man" and her hesitant interaction with him: "the skittish horses of his eyes" as he "crossed the street for [her] two dollars," her holding "out the stiff bills" to him "as if she were holding him / at gunpoint," her wanting to analogize their exchange for him in the language and performance of metaphor.

Such emotional texture as this investment in more poetic language offers stands out against the matter-of-fact narrative the poet gives in the beginning of the preacher's well-practiced piety. And this texture not only deepens what seems a simple poem, but it points to a more complicated, more human engagement with grace. Because it's not as simple to understand and practice the principle of grace as merely putting on business attire to garner others' trust, talking a good game, and calling forth tears as you manipulate an audience into awakening a sensationalized, commodified faith. Rather it means making yourself vulnerable to others' language, to others' needs and then responding in kind— by sharing your own language and desires. It means performing with others the "high-rise routine" of human kinship. It means stumbling and gaining experience and making that experience available to the world, all of which the poet does in "Acrobats." Because even though, after offering her money to the man, she withholds her language ("I wanted to tell him," "I wanted to say"), something that might have bridged the gap between them, she then tries to fill this gap and expand her empathy, her human reach by revising the experience with her poem. In my mind such a narrative move is a greater indication of the storyteller's character, a more powerful extension of grace, and a greater means of persuasion than any scripted, televangelized sermon ever could be.

Tyler Chadwick

His word, more than his face, remains—

In late November 2011, Dad called my siblings and me to his parents' house so we could find something in their estate to take as a memorial of their influence in our lives. Sifting for potential nuggets in their mote- and memory-dense basement, I found Grandpa's old scriptures boxed away with a stack of LDS devotional books: his pocket-sized, Armed Forces edition of *Principles of the Gospel* (1943), inscribed in his younger self's handwriting "LDS Army booklet received Feb. 1945"; his pocket-sized, Armed Forces edition of The Book of Mormon (1943), inscribed "Property of Don L. Chadwick ~ Acquired at LDS soldier's [sic] meetings in Tokyo, Japan, January 6, 1946"; and his triple combination with black, faux leather cover and red-edged pages (1957), inscribed "Don L. Chadwick Afton, Wyo." Each book is well-worn, but The Book of Mormon especially: its bent and frayed cover is heavily taped to the binding strip on the outside and, on the inside, to the book's first and last pages; its leaves are amber with age and the oil from Grandpa's repeated touch; and the index concludes (ironically enough) with the references for "War," the final pages of the book having fallen or been torn out or become subject to some such moment of loss at some point during Grandpa's life narrative. Although the other books are a bit less heavily worn, none of them really have lasting value beyond what they convey to me of Grandpa's habits of being—the characteristic ways in which he inhabited and interacted with the material and immaterial worlds, including language, the earth, and his faith.

Thumbing through the books—especially The Book of Mormon—raising the mustiness and rot of decaying paper and glue, trying to make out the few notes Grandpa had scribbled in pencil in the margins, I tried to inhabit the language as maybe Grandpa had done during that post-war soldiers' meeting in Tokyo or during a homesick night on his bunk while he waited for the ship to return him to his young wife or years later when he maybe pulled the book from a drawer, opened it to a random page, and mulled over the image of God he found staring at him through the words. Beside 1 Nephi 22:11, a younger version of the man I knew had penciled a question mark lightly in the margin. The question, it seems, is about an image in the verse: a God reaching down from his exalted place and making bare his arm in the eyes of all nations, an embodied God revealing his body, his promise of salvation, to humanity in an act of unquestionable grace. I imagine Grandpa re-reading the verse, wondering over its meaning, reaching for some answer to a question that he carried with him like this small book. And in response? Another question, another point of uncertainty in a time when the war had ended but when War was really far from over. So he lifted his pencil from the desk and touched a question mark in the margins: a token that he had been there, that he had inhabited those verses, that language; that he had weighed himself against their meaning, their promise, and somehow found himself and his knowledge wanting.

I may or may not be puzzling over this more than he ever did. The question mark is, after all, barely a mark on the page. But it's a question mark nonetheless and I've returned to it many times in my pondering. It seems so out of place in a book to which millions of people, myself included, turn for answers. But maybe that's why it's so light in the margins: Grandpa didn't want to appear the doubter. The central question it calls to mind, though, relates to the central question of the verse, and really, of Christianity: who is this God? For whom is he reaching? Does he bare that arm for me?

And then I think of the drifter I met some years ago on an early morning run through the streets just off Ogden's east bench. As we moved closer to each other, he hesitated and moved toward me. I became a little skittish because I don't normally get approached by people while I'm running and I wasn't really in the best neighborhood. But he didn't move to take anything from me; he wasn't threatening me. All he offered were thirteen words that have stuck in my mind: "Have you necessarily taken the time," he asked, "to find out what grace is for?"

I didn't stop to answer, even though he swiveled on his foot as I passed and waited for a response. I just turned the next corner, anxious to get out of the rain that had begun falling, to wipe my glasses free of the drops, to slip into dry clothes. But the question stuck. And I've run my mind over it for years, sort of like I keep returning to an imagined image of Grandpa sitting at a desk or a table on his lunch hour or during a slow patch in the office he occupied after the war; or, alternately, laying on his bunk in dawn's blur, feeling his way through Nephi's discourse on salvation, stopping when his mind catches on an image— a metonymy—that strikes him as significant: a God baring his arm before his people. But for whatever reason, he can't quite parse it, can't quite figure out what this bare arm means. And as he reaches for his pencil, I see the warm flesh of his wrist exposed from the end of his shirt and, through the mark he leaves on the page, I sense him reaching to grasp what abides beyond each translucent verse.

Tyler Chadwick

221

ENDNOTES

Introduction

Neil Aitken, "Burials," *Fire in the Pasture* (El Cerrito, CA: Peculiar Pages, 2011) 3. Originally published in Neil's book *The Lost Country of Sight* (Tallahassee, FL: Anhinga Press, 2008) 20.

S.P. Bailey, "Ripple Rock," *Fire in the Pasture* 27. Originally published in *Dialogue: A Journal of Mormon Thought* 43.3 (2010): 167.

Laura Stott, "Across the Mojave Desert," *Fire in the Pasture* 398. Originally published in *Literature and Belief* 31.1 (2011): 108–9.

"Alex Caldiero's two line lyric": Alex Caldiero, "It occurs to me," *Fire in the Pasture* 82. Originally published in *I Am Not Only: only Bruce Conner did not say this* (Salt Lake City: Alex Caldiero, 2008) 1.

Lisa Bickmore, "Panis Angelicus," *Fire in the Pasture* 52.

John Talbot, "An Expulsion Exclogue," *Fire in the Pasture* 419–24. Originally published in *Literary Imagination* 12.1 (2010): 68–72, as "Eclogue I: Virgil."

N. Colwell Snell, "Vienna 1965," *Fire in the Pasture* 388. Originally published in *Weber Studies* 23.3 (2007).

From "what poet Patricia Karamesines" to "language makers": Patricia Karamesines, "Introduction to the Mysteries (or How to Read a Poem)," *Fire in the Pasture* 245–46.

Prologue

Billy Collins, "Introduction to Poetry," *The Apple that Astonished Paris* (Fayetteville: University of Arkansas Press, 1988) 58.

Patricia Karamesines, "Introduction to the Mysteries (or How to Read a Poem),"

Fire in the Pasture 245–46.

To follow what calls—

From "Walt Whitman" to "out of pocket": See Justin Kaplan, *Walt Whitman: A Life* (New York: Perennial Classics) 198.

"Five more official editions over the next twenty-six years": The first edition of *Leaves of Grass* was published in 1855. Revised and expanded editions were published in the following years: 1856, 1860, 1867, 1871, and 1881. See Ed Folsom and Kenneth M. Price, eds., "Published Works: Books by Whitman," *The Walt Whitman Archive* (2000), www.whitmanarchive.org. Accessed 6 June 2013.

"*Leaves of Grass* . . . falls broadly within the georgic tradition": For a broad discussion of the "georgic inheritance in American poetry" and how Whitman fits into that, see Margaret Ronda, "Georgic Disenchantment in American Poetry," *Genre* 46.1 (2013): 57–78.

From "Camerados" to "as long as we live": These lines come from the last stanza of "Song of the Open Road," *Leaves of Grass* (New York: Barnes & Noble Books, 2004) 208. The entire poem spans from 196–208. All subsequent references to "Song of the Open Road" come from this edition.

Note for Entry 2

Alan Rex Mitchell, "Joseph's Soliloquy," *Fire in the Pasture* 286–87. Originally published in *The Road to Carthage* (Vernon, UT: Greenjacket Books, 2010).

Howard Schwartz, "The *Tzohar*," *Tree of Souls: The Mythology of Judaism* (Oxford: Oxford University Press, 2004) 85–8.

"The *tzohar*'s appearance in Mahonri Moriancumer's story": In Ether 2:23, the Lord asks Mahonri Moriancumer, "What will yet that I should do that ye may have light in your vessels? For behold, ye cannot have windows, for they will be dashed in pieces." Verse 23 footnote *a*, which appears beside "windows" in the

2013 LDS version of the text, references Genesis 6:16 where the Lord tells Noah (as recorded in the King James Version), "A window shalt thou make to the ark." Schwartz and others render this phrase, "Put the tzohar in the ark" (85, 86–7).

Note for Entry 3

Melissa Dalton Bradford, "Bottled Fruit," *Fire in the Pasture* 131–32. Originally published in *Irreantum* 12.2 (2010): 100–101.

Proving Rocks

"The long brown path . . . leading wherever I choose": This line is from the first stanza of the poem (found on page 196 of the quoted edition).

From "In 'Song of the Open Road" to "give them shape": All quoted material comes from the first three sections of "Song of the Open Road" (found on pages 196–98 of the quoted edition).

William Clayton, "Come, Come Ye Saints," *Hymns of the Church of Jesus Christ of Latter-day Saints* (Salt Lake City: The Church of Jesus Christ of Latter-day Saints, 1985) #30 (37–8).

Elizabeth Fetzer Bates, "Pioneer Children Sang as They Walked," *The Children's Songbook of The Church of Jesus Christ of Latter-day Saints* (Salt Lake City: The Church of Jesus Christ of Latter-day Saints, 2005) 214.

From "the very stuff of life" to "companionship": Adam Miller, *Rube Goldberg Machines: Essays in Mormon Theology* (Draper, UT: Greg Kofford Books, 2012) Kindle locations 187–202.

From "the secret" to "open air": These lines are from the second stanza of the sixth section of "Song of the Open Road" (found on page 199 of the quoted edition).

Note for Entry 4

S.P. Bailey, "Ripple Rock," *Fire in the Pasture* 27. Originally published in *Dialogue: A Journal of Mormon Thought* 43.3 (2010): 167.

Philip White, "The River," *Fire in the Pasture* 466–67. Originally published in *The Cincinnati Review* 5.1 (2008).

Pooling and surging and purling and cleaving and cleaving—

"The numbing noise of business": Gideon Burton, "Good Friday," *Open Source Sonnets* (6 Apr. 2012), opensourcesonnets.blogspot.com. Accessed 25 Sept. 2012.

"When the whole body is one sense, and imbibes delight through every pore": Henry David Thoreau, *Walden; or, Life in the Woods* (Boston: Ticknor and Fields, 1854) 140.

Note for Entry 5

Joe Plicka, "True Love," *Fire in the Pasture* 358–59. Originally published in *Inscape* (Winter 2006).

"The paintings of Utah artist J. Kirk Richards": To get a sense of Kirk's work and to view images of the paintings I reference throughout *Field Notes on Language and Kinship*, see his website at jkirkrichards.com.

Note for Entry 6

From "As Tom F. Driver notes" to "language and culture": Tom F. Driver, *Liberating Rites: Understanding the Transformative Power of Ritual* (Boulder, CO: Westview Press, 1998) 6.

Laura Stott, "Across the Mojave Desert," Fire in the Pasture 398. Originally published in *Literature and Belief* 31.1 (2011): 108–9.

Note for Entry 7

"Māori words": Unless otherwise noted, translations of Māori words are from the *Māori Dictionary* found online at www.maoridictionary.co.nz.

From "In Māori mythology" to "made the world": Rāwiri Taonui, "Ranginui—the Sky," *Te Ara—The Encyclopedia of New Zealand* (Manatū Taonga: Ministry for Culture and Heritage, 22 Sept. 2012), www.teara.govt.nz. Accessed 7 June 2013.

Michael R. Collings, "At Midnight," *Fire in the Pasture* 114. Originally published in *In the Void: Poems of Science Fiction, Myth and Fantasy, & Horror* (Rockville, MD: Borgo/Wildside Press, 2009) 129–30.

Note for Entry 8

David Passey, "The Road to Vegas," *Fire in the Pasture* 336.

Note for Entry 9

Kristen Eliason, "arms upon arms to an earth," *Fire in the Pasture* 171. Originally published in *Diagram* 9.1 (2009): 8.

"Buddhist Dictionary housed at *Orientalia*": Ron Epstein, ed., "Wayplace," *Buddhism A to Z* (Burlingame, CA: Buddhist Text Translation Society, 1992), *Orientalia: Eastern Philosophy, Religion, and Culture* (Eurasia Academic Publishers, 2004), www.orientalia.org. Accessed 14 Apr. 2009.

From "Trent Johnson . . . died in a 2005 accident on Gunlock Reservoir": Associated Press, "Body of Dixie Man Found at Gunlock," *Deseret News* [Salt Lake City, UT] 2 June 2005, www.deseretnews.com. Accessed 7 June 2013.

Note for Entries 10 & 11

From "Legend has it" to "World of Light": Rāwiri Taonui, "Ngāpuhi—Canoes," *Te Ara—The Encyclopedia of New Zealand* (Manatū Taonga: Ministry for Culture and Heritage, 22 Sept. 2012), www.teara.govt.nz. Accessed 7 June 2013.

Translation of "*Te Kohanga o Te Tai Tokerau*" from Sandy Myhre, "The Hokianga," *The Northland Age* 28 Dec. 2012, www.northlandage.co.nz. Accessed 7 June 2013.

"Puddles of deep, sweet silence": Sarah Dunster, "Taxi," *Fire in the Pasture* 154.

Note for Entry 12

Jim Papworth, "Postcard," *Fire in the Pasture* 326. Originally published in *Perspective* 3.1 (2003): 59.

Note for Entries 13 & 14

David Nielsen, "My Daughter's Favorite Bedtime Story," *Fire in the Pasture* 301. Originally published in *Willow Springs* 57 (2006).

"Two line lyric by Alex Caldiero": Alex Caldiero, "It occurs to me," *Fire in the Pasture* 82. Originally published in *I Am Not Only: only Bruce Conner did not say this* (Salt Lake City: Alex Caldiero, 2008) 1.

Koru Sonnets: Koru 2

"Māui's hook in the tongue": "A central story about Māui tells of how he fished up the North Island of New Zealand. The South Island is referred to as *Te Waka-a-Māui*, or Māui's canoe. Rakiura (Stewart Island) is the canoe's anchor stone and it is said that Māui stood at the peninsula at Kaikōua while he hauled up his prized catch." Te Ahukaramū Charles Royal, "First Peoples in Māori Tradition—Māui," *Te Ara—The Encyclopedia of New Zealand* (Manatū Taonga: Ministry for Culture and Heritage, 22 Sept. 2012), www.teara.govt.nz. Accessed 7 June 2013.

Weaving Ethnography with Alex, Some Māori, and Mormonism

From "At the 2012 conference" to "assumptions and institutions": My report on this conference presentation can be found at fireinthepasture.org/2012/situating-sonosophy/.

"Alex's 2010 'Poetarium' performance": A video recording of this performance is available in five parts on YouTube: "Intro to the Poetarium @ 2010 Utah Arts Festival," "Poetarium Part 1 @ 2010 Utah Arts Festival," "Poetarium Part 2 @ 2010 Utah Arts Festival," "Poetarium Part 3 @ 2010 Utah Arts Festival," "Poetarium Part 4 @ 2010 Utah Arts Festival," *YouTube* (the69lover69, 27 June 2010), www.youtube.com. Accessed 9 June 2013.

From "an archetypal performer" to "upside-down": Dwight Conquergood, "Poetics, Play, Process, and Power: The Performative Turn in Anthropology," *Text and Performance Quarterly* 1 (1989): 83.

"Performing as a moral act": Dwight Conquergood, "Performing as a Moral Act: Ethical Dimensions of the Ethnography of Performance," *Literature in Performance* 5.2 (1985): 1.

From "the possibilities of dialogue" to "to change us": Eugene England, "The Possibility of Dialogue," *Dialogues with Myself* (Salt Lake City: Orion Books, 1984) 39–40.

From "cultural performance" to "everyday life": Norman K. Denzin, *Performance Ethnography: Critical Pedagogy and the Politics of Culture* (Los Angeles: Sage Publications, 2003) 8.

From "Performance theorist" to "a different performer": Richard Schechner, *Performance Studies: An Introduction* (2nd ed) (New York: Routledge, 2006) 28.

From "More than just mere imitation" to "the truth of their experience": Diana Taylor, "Translating Performance," *The Performance Studies Reader* edited by Henry Bial (New York: Routledge, 2004) 381.

From "In their discussion" to "(integrity and sincerity)": Tuwhakairiora Williams and David Robinson, "Social Capital and Philanthropy in Maori Society," *The In-*

ternational Journal of Not-for-Profit Law 6.2 (2004), www.icnl.org. Accessed 27 May 2012.

From "In the first paragraph" to "into each other": Conquergood, "Performing as a Moral Act" 1.

From "Glassie confesses" to "make life comprehensible": Henry Glassie, *Passing the Time in Ballymenone: Culture and History of an Ulster Community* (Philadelphia: University of Pennsylvania Press, 1982) xvi.

From "it helps" to "not always pretty": Conquergood, "Performing as a Moral Act" 2.

From "to make what Conquergood calls" to "without, of course, losing sight of the self": Quotations from "Performing as a Moral Act" 4–10.

From "what Conquergood elsewhere calls" to "as bodies in the world": Dwight Conquergood, "Rethinking Ethnography: Towards a Critical Cultural Politics," *Communication Monographs* 58 (1991): 181.

From "what Denzin describes" to "readers and viewers": Norman K. Denzin, *Interpretive Ethnography: Ethnographic Practices for the 21st Century* (Thousand Oaks, CA: SAGE Publications, 1997) 39.

From "Elyse Lamm Pineau" to "kinesthetically as well as intellectually": Elyse Lamm Pineau, "Critical Performative Pedagogy: Fleshing Out the Politics of Liberatory Education," *Teaching Performance Studies* edited by Nathan Stuck and Cynthia Wimmer (Carbondale: Southern Illinois UP, 2002) 49; italics mine.

From "moving to meet 'people'" to "point of departure and return": Dwight Conquergood, "Performance Studies: Interventions and Radical Research," *The Performance Studies Reader* edited by Henry Bial (New York: Routledge, 2004) 373.

Tracie Morris, "Love in 2010," *Sexualities and Politics in the Americas*, Special issue of *e-misférica* 2.2 (2005), hemisphericinstitute.org/journal/2_2/. Accessed 8 June 2013.

Alex Caldiero, "Poetry: Alex Caldiero. [Seeing a Body]," *YouTube* (Northern-UtahPeace, 31 Oct. 2009), youtube.com. Accessed 28 May 2012.

Note for Part 3: Panis Angelicus

From "The phrase" to "Eucharist": I drew this information from two different sources: 1) Michael Martin, "*Sacris Solemniis*: At This Our Solemn Feast," Thesaurus Precum Latinarum: *Treasury of Latin Prayers* (Michael Martin, 2013), www.preces-latinae.org. Accessed 9 June 2013. 2) Francis Mershman, "Feast of Corpus Christi," *The Catholic Encyclopedia* (Vol. 4) (New York: Robert Appleton Company, 1908), www.newadvent.org/cathen. Accessed 9 June 2013.

Translation of "*Panis angelicus / Fit panis hominum*" from "*Panis angelicus*," *Choral Public Domain Library (ChoralWiki)* (31 Mar. 2013), www.choralwiki.org. Accessed 9 June 2013.

Lisa Bickmore, "Panis angelicus," *Fire in the Pasture* 52.

Note for Entry 16

Elizabeth Pinborough, "A Shaker Sister's Hymnal," *Fire in the Pasture* 352–56. Originally published in *Dialogue: A Journal of Mormon Thought* 42.2 (2009): 97–101.

Note for Entry 17

Lisa Bickmore, "Panis Angelicus," *Fire in the Pasture* 52.

John Talbot, "An Expulsion Exclogue," *Fire in the Pasture* 419–24. Originally published in *Literary Imagination* 12.1 (2010): 68–72, as "Eclogue I: Virgil."

Note for Entry 18

George Herbert, "Easter Wings," *The Temple: Sacred Poems and Private Ejaculations*

(London: T. Buck and R. Daniel [University of Cambridge], 1638) 34–5. Available online via *The Internet Archive* (2006), archive.org. Accessed 9 June 2013.

Lance Larsen, "To the Lost One-Third," *Fire in the Pasture* 256. Originally published in *Backyard Alchemy* (Tampa: University of Tampa Press, 2009) 56.

Note for Entry 19

Timothy Liu, "Genesis 29:20," *Fire in the Pasture* 266.

Note for Entries 20 & 21

Susan Elizabeth Howe, "Both the Fragrance and the Color," *Fire in the Pasture* 225–26.

Sharlee Mullins Glenn, "Somewhere," *Fire in the Pasture* 188–89. Originally published in *Segullah* 1.2 (Fall 2005).

Note for Entry 22

Lance Larsen, "Why Do You Keep Putting Animals in Your Poems?," *Fire in the Pasture* 257. Originally published in *The Best American Poetry 2009* edited by David Wagoner and David Lehman (New York City: Scribner Poetry, 2009) 68–9.

Note for Entries 23, 24, & 25

Marilyn Nielson, "Sheep," *Fire in the Pasture* 310. Originally published in *BYU Studies* 44.2 (2005): 176.

Lisa Bickmore, "Dog Aria," *Fire in the Pasture* 51.

Neil Aitken, "Burials," Fire in the Pasture (El Cerrito, CA: Peculiar Pages, 2011)

3. Originally published in Neil's book *The Lost Country of Sight* (Tallahassee, FL: Anhinga Press, 2008) 20.

There was a moment we understood—

From "the heaven and the earth" to "fishes of the sea": Doctrine and Covenants 29:24.

The long notes, impossibly long—

"In her performance of the poem (available on YouTube)": Lisa Bickmore, "Bite Size Poet for May 2010: Lisa Bickmore Performs 'Dog Aria,'" *YouTube* (UTArtsandMuseums, 29 Apr. 2010), www.youtube.com. Accessed 9 June 2013.

Note for Entry 26

Matthew James Babcock, "Moose Remembered," *Fire in the Pasture* 13. Originally published in *Terrain* 25 (2010).

Note for Entries 27 & 28

Michael Hicks, "Family Tree," *Fire in the Pasture* 218. Originally published in *Dialogue: A Journal of Mormon Thought* 38.4 (2005): 206–7.

Jon Ogden, "Prayer Cap," *Fire in the Pasture* 314. Originally published in *Inscape* (Winter 2006).

Note for Entry 29

"Some self portraits poet Holly Welker has composed": As mentioned, one of Holly's self portraits is included in *Fire in the Pasture* on pages 455–56: "Self-Portrait as Burnt Offering." Others include her poem, "Self-Portrait as Someone

Who Looks Exactly Like Me," *The Spoon River Poetry Review* 30.2 (2005); her essay, "Self-Portrait as Critic with Body," *The Iowa Review* 33.2 (2003): 58–92; and her MFA thesis, "Self-Portrait as Essayist: Twenty-four Ways of Looking at an Essay" (University of Iowa, 2002).

"In the simmer and slow furnace / of morning": Mark D. Bennion, "Compass," *Psalm & Selah: A Poetic Journey through the Book of Mormon* (Woodsboro, MD: Parables, 2009) 13–14.

Note for Part 5: Eden's Half-light

From "in her poem" to "thighs": Sharon Olds, "Monarchs," *Satan Says* (Pittsburgh: University of Pittsburgh Press, 1980) 33.

"At least one critic has called it pornographic": Helen Vendler "once labeled Sharon Olds's seemingly autobiographical narratives of sexuality and family life 'pornographic.'" Dinitia Smith, *The New York Times* 22 Nov. 1997, www.nytimes.com. Accessed 10 June 2013.

"I sing the body electric": Walt Whitman, "I Sing the Body Electric," *Leaves of Grass* (New York: Barnes & Noble Books, 2004) 132–41.

Note for Entry 30

Jim Richards, "Cleave," *Fire in the Pasture* 376. Originally published in *Literature and Belief* 23.1 (2003).

Note for Entries 31, 32, & 33

Will Bishop, "When I Do Go On My Honeymoon," *Fire in the Pasture* 57. Originally published in *The Fob Bible* edited by Eric W Jepson, et al (El Cerrito, CA: Peculiar Pages, 2009) 11.

Elaine Wright Christensen, "Sermon on Manchac Swamp," *Fire in the Pasture* 107.

Originally published in *Encore: Prize Poems of the NFSPS 2000* edited by Budd Powell (Dallas, TX: Great Impressions, 2000).

Danny Nelson, "Creation," *The Fob Bible* edited by Eric W Jepson, et al (El Cerrito, CA: Peculiar Pages, 2009) 3. Available online via *Plain and Precious Parts from The Fob Bible* (Peculiar Pages, 2009), b10mediaworx.com. Accessed 11 June 2013.

Like passing the sacrament—

From "a paradox" to "atop the marriage bed": See Anonymous, "When Virgins Collide," *Sunstone* 150 (July 2008): 31–4.

"The union of 'the spirit and the body'": Doctrine and Covenants 88:15.

Praying for roothold—

From "[t]he world is charged" to "'smell[ing]' of human sweat": Gerard Manley Hopkins, "God's Grandeur," *Poems of Gerard Manley Hopkins Now First Published* (London: Humphrey Milford, 1918) 26. Available online via Project Gutenberg (26 Aug. 2007), www.gutenberg.org. Accessed 11 June 2013.

"In her verbal performance of her poem (available on YouTube)": Elaine Wright Christensen, "Bite Size 2.0 for November 2010: Elaine Wright Christensen Performs 'Sermon on Manchac Swamp,'" *YouTube* (UtahArtsandMuseums, 16 Nov. 2010), www.youtube.com. Accessed 11 June 2013.

Always the procreant urge—

From "procreant urge of creation" to "out of the dimness": Walt Whitman, "Song of Myself," *Leaves of Grass* (New York: Barnes & Noble Books, 2004) 55.

From "As Eliza R. Snow reminds us" to "I've a Mother there": "O My Father," *Hymns of the Church of Jesus Christ of Latter-day Saints* (Salt Lake City: The Church of Jesus Christ of Latter-day Saints, 1985) #292 (317–18).

From "sociality" to "eternal glory": Doctrine and Covenants 130:2.

"God, whose name is Eternal": Moses 7:35.

"The highest 'order of the priesthood [meaning the new and everlasting covenant of marriage'": Doctrine and Covenants 131:2.

"A continuation of the [pair's] seeds": Doctrine and Covenants 132:19.

From "As Book of Mormon" to "his children": 1 Nephi 11:17.

From "as Brigham Young taught" to "from eternity to eternity": Brigham Young, "Marriage Relations of Bishops and Deacons," *Journal of Discourses* (Vol. 2) (Liverpool: F. D. Richards [Latter-day Saints' Book Depot], 1855) 90.

"Continuation of . . . lives": Doctrine and Covenants 132:22.

Note for Entry 34

From "Such counsel is based" to "will damn us": See Matthew 5:27–30, 3 Nephi 12:27–30, and Doctrine and Covenants 42:22–26.

From "From this perspective" to "anything like unto thinking about sex": See Doctrine and Covenants 59:6.

Lucille Clifton, "lorena," *The Terrible Stories* (Rochester, NY: BOA Editions, Ltd., 1996) 55.

Sharon Olds, "The Language of the Brag," *Satan Says* (Pittsburgh: University of Pittsburgh Press, 1980) 44–5.

From "The word *epic*" to "word, story, or poem": "Epic," *Online Etymology Dictionary* (Douglas Harper, 2013), www.etymonline.com. Accessed 1 Aug. 2013.

Walt Whitman, "Song of Myself," *Leaves of Grass* (New York: Barnes and Noble Books, 2004) 53–125.

Allen Ginsberg, "Howl," *Howl and Other Poems* (San Francisco: City Lights Books, [1956] 2001) 9–26.

From "as young Mormons" to "the presence of my parents": See, for instance, this Mormon Messages video produced by the Church and addressed specifically to Mormon youth: "Chastity: What are the Limits?" *YouTube* (MormonMessagesYouth, 26 May 2011), www.youtube.com. Accessed 1 Aug. 2013.

From "my thoughts" to "condemn me": See Alma 12:14.

"As I've noted elsewhere": See especially "Always the procreant urge—."

"A Latter-day Saint theology of desire": For an insightful discussion of how the erotic functions within the context of LDS theology, see Cetti Cherniak's two-part article titled "The Theology of Desire" from *Dialogue: A Journal of Mormon Thought*. Part I appeared in volume 40.1 (2007): 1–42, Part II in 40:2 (2007): 1–46.

Javen Tanner, "Eden," *Fire in the Pasture* 430–31. Originally published in *Curses for Your Sake* (New York: Mormon Artists Group, 2006) 1–2.

"He finds there": Based on Javen's biological sex, Edenic mythology, and Mormonism's sanction of heterosexual relationships, I'm assuming the poem's speaker is male, although it could also productively be read as female. But that reading is for another essay.

From "Speaking to the intersection" to "a form a making love": Alicia Ostriker, *Dancing at the Devil's Party: Essays on Poetry, Politics, and the Erotic* (Ann Arbor: University of Michigan Press, 2000) 38–9.

"The serpent being a widely-regarded symbol for both Satan (the Great Antagonist) and Christ": See, for instance, Andrew C. Skinner, "Serpent Symbols and Salvation in the Ancient Near East and the Book of Mormon," *Journal of Book of Mormon Studies* 10.2 (2001): 42–55, 70–71.

Note for Part 6: Bethesda

From "Just north" to "their next chance at a miracle": See John 5:2–9.

Note for Entry 35

Doug Talley, *Adam's Dream: Poems for a Latter Day* (Woodsboro, MD: Parables, 2011). My original review of the book can be accessed online via the *Association for Mormon Letters Discussion Board* (Association for Mormon Letters, 5 Apr. 2012), forums.mormonletters.org. Accessed 11 June 2013.

Giving the Beauty of Holiness a Tongue

"A proverb of Solomon": Proverbs 3:5–6.

"They settled on Malachi 3": Malachi 3:10–12.

From "Brigham Young acknowledged" to "produced by men": Brigham Young, *Discourses of Brigham Young* compiled and edited by John A. Widstoe (Salt Lake City: Deseret News Press, 1925) 261–62.

From "Plato" to "mere words": Plato, *Gorgias* translated by W. R. Lamb, in *Plato in Twelve Volumes* (Vol. 3) (Cambridge, MA: Harvard University Press, 1967) 463a–b.

From "words are a matter of faith" to "providing service to others": "It is by words, instead of exerting his [sic] physical powers, with which every being works when he works by faith." *Lectures on Faith* (American Fork, UT: Covenant Communications, 2000) 69 (Lecture 7:3).

From "The autumnal decline" to "Amen": These lines appear on pages 85–114 of *Adam's Dream*. Included in full with Doug's permission.

"The beauty of holiness begs a tongue": Talley xi.

"Hymn of the Morning Star": Talley 3. Included in full with Doug's permission.

From "As the Lord told Emma Smith" to "their heads": Doctrine and Covenants 25:12.

From "In his *Defense of Poetry*" to "whence or why": Percy Bysshe Shelley, *A Defense of Poetry* Boston: Ginn & Company, 1891) 11–12. Available online via The Internet Archive (2005), archive.org. Accessed 11 June 2013.

"Latter-day Aesthetic": Talley 78–9. Also *Fire in the Pasture* 429. Included in full with Doug's permission.

From "natural mode of speech" to "western United States": James Dickey, *Babel to Byzantium: Poets and Poetry Now* (New York: Ecco Press, 1981) 139.

"Perspective on Greater Eternities": Talley 22.

"Parable for the Pulse of the Wrist": Talley 31–2. Also *Fire in the Pasture* 426. Long excerpt included with Doug's permission.

Note for Entry 36

"The story in the Gospel of Luke": Luke 19:1–6.

N. Colwell Snell, "Vienna 1965," *Fire in the Pasture* 388. Originally published in *Weber Studies* 23.3 (2007).

Note for Entries 37 & 38

Sally Stratford, "Inheritance," *Fire in the Pasture* 400. Originally published in *Dialogue: A Journal of Mormon Thought* 36.3 (2003): 52.

Danielle Beazer Dubrasky, "Legacy," *Fire in the Pasture* 141. Originally published in *Dialogue: A Journal of Mormon Thought* 34.3–4 (2001): 56.

Note for Entry 39

Melissa Dalton-Bradford, "Pietà," *Fire in the Pasture* 130. Originally published in *Irreantum* 12.2 (2010): 94–5.

Deja Earley, "I Teach Six-Year-Olds about Jesus in Sunday School," *Fire in the Pasture* 157. Originally published in *Dialogue: A Journal of Mormon Thought* 40.3 (2007): 171.

Will Reger, "Mass Transit Madonna," *Fire in the Pasture* 373.

Note for Entry 40

Arwen Taylor, "*Lingua Doctrinae*," *Fire in the Pasture* 444–45. Originally published in *The Fob Bible* edited by Eric W Jepson, et al (El Cerrito, CA: Peculiar Pages, 2009) 199–200.

Note for Entry 41

Jonathon Penny, "Confession, after Battle," *Fire in the Pasture* 347.

Note for Part 7: The Gods Step Out of Their Hiding Place

Joanna Brooks, "When the Mormons of Orange County Become Shintoists," *Fire in the Pasture* 68.

"All spirit is matter": Doctrine and Covenants 131:7.

From "by going from a small capacity" to "sit enthroned": Joseph Smith, Jr., "The King Follett Discourse" edited by Stan Larson, *BYU Studies* 18.2 (1978): 8.

Note for Entry 42

Marie Brian, "Spindrift," *Fire in the Pasture* 64. Originally published in *Segullah*

2.1 (Spring 2006).

Note for Entries 43, 44, & 45

Claire Åkebrand, "October Plush," *Fire in the Pasture* 8. Originally published in *Splash of Red* (12 Feb. 2010).

Sara Blaisdell, "Ophelia," *Fire in the Pasture* 62. Originally published in *Literature and Belief* 23.2 (2004).

From "map-maker Jerry Gretzinger" to "(as of 2012)": Dan Colman, "Jerry's Map: An Amazing Half Century Act of Imagination," *Open Culture* (Open Culture, LLC, 30 Aug. 2011), www.openculture.com. Accessed 11 June 2013.

Glen Nelson, "Barbie Love," *Fire in the Pasture* 299.

The Word that says everything—

"It's always other people who die": "Duchamp, Marcel (1887–1968)," *Oxford Dictionary of Modern and Contemporary Art* (2nd Ed.) edited by Ian Chilvers and John R. Glaves-Smith (New York: Oxford University Press, 2009).

From "Stop, Christian" to "life in death": Samuel Taylor Coleridge, "Epitaph," *The Complete Poetical Works of Samuel Taylor Coleridge* (Oxford: Clarendon Press, 1912) 491–92. Available online via *Project Gutenberg* (11 June 2009), www.-gutenberg.org. Accessed 11 June 2013.

Your arms are open to something—

From "Shakespeare's lady" to "music vows": William Shakespeare, *Hamlet* 3.1.134–35 in the Harvard Classics Edition (1909–14) available on *Bartleby.com* (Bartleby.com, 2001), www.bartleby.com. Accessed 16 Aug. 2013.

"Dead men's fingers": *Hamlet* 4.7.184 in the Harvard Classics Edition (1909–

14) available on *Bartleby.com* (Bartleby.com, 2001), www.bartleby.com. Accessed 16 Aug. 2013.

From "Speaking to the ways" to "domain of tradition": Walter Benjamin, "The Work of Art in the Age of Mechanical Reproduction," *Marxists Internet Archive* (Feb. 2005), www.marxists.org. Accessed 11 June 2013.

Note for Entry 46

"A wholesome tongue is a tree of life": Proverbs 15:4. For the alternate translations I mention, see "Proverbs 15:4," *Bible Hub* (Biblos.com, 2013), biblehub.com. Accessed 11 June 2013.

Casualene Meyer, "Why you should not bite your tongue (didactic poem #2)," *Fire in the Pasture* 282.

Gideon Burton, "Salt and Blood," *Fire in the Pasture* 74. Originally published on *Open Source Sonnets* (3 Dec. 2010), opensourcesonnets.blogspot.com. Accessed 11 June 2013.

The Tongue as Tree of Life

"The Makers needed a plan": See Abraham 4.

"They watched the universe unfold in their minds": See Abraham 4:18.

"Hence John: In the beginning was the Word": John 1:1.

"The Makers' plurality": The use of "Gods" in Abraham 4 & 5 suggests a coterie of creative Beings.

From "The Makers are a Community" to "procreative work": See Doctrine and Covenants 130:2 and 131:1–4.

"The plurality of the Makers' creations": See for starters Doctrine and Covenants

76:24 and Moses 1:33.

"The Makers build things from materials extant in the universe": See Abraham 3:24.

"Creation unfolds in an eternal round": See for instance Doctrine and Covenants 35:1.

"We can emulate our Parents and become Makers ourselves": See Joseph Smith, Jr., "The King Follett Discourse."

"The Makers have bodies of flesh and bone": See especially Doctrine and Covenants 130:22.

From "A thing, at its root" to "a being": "Thing," *Online Etymology Dictionary* (Douglas Harper, 2013), www.etymonline.com. Accessed 11 June 2013.

"In a series of poems published in his 2010 collection": These poems include "So I know" (37–8), "Whimper" (39–40), "Mute" (41–2), "Troubled times" (43–4), "Terra incognita" (45–6), "This day as a version of the last" (47), "In the Loop" (48), and "Shorn" (49). All appear in *Words for Empty and Words for Full* (Pittsburgh: University of Pittsburgh Press, 2010).

From "aftermath" to "a destructive event": "Aftermath," *Online Etymology Dictionary* (Douglas Harper, 2013), www.etymonline.com. Accessed 11 June 2013.

"Cho's multimedia manifesto": The written portion: Cho Seung-Hui, "Seung Hui Cho's 'Manifesto'" (PDF), *SchoolShooters.info* (Peter Langman, 2012), www.schoolshooters.info. Accessed 11 June 2013. Portions of the video: Cho Seung-Hui, "Seung-Hui Cho Full Video Virginia Tech Shooter," *YouTube* (Babylon616, 24 Apr. 2007), www.youtube.com. Accessed 11 June 2013.

From "Satan's descendants" to "Rapists": "Seung Hui Cho's 'Manifesto'" 1.

"The boy 'felt / that he was nothing'": Hicok 48.

"He ultimately 'unworded' himself": Hicok 37.

From "A shadow under the awning of his cap" to "let nothing": Hicok 41–2.

From "Many who remember Cho" to "conversation with him": Alex Johnson, et al, "High School Classmates Say Gunman was Bullied," *NBCNews.com* 19 Apr. 2007, www.nbcnews.com. Accessed 11 June 2013.

From "*The Onion*" to "to hell": "F—— Everything, Nation Reports," *The Onion: America's Finest News Source* 14 Dec. 2012, www.theonion.com. Accessed 11 June 2013.

"The verb means to copulate with, to thrust, to strike, to push": "F——," *Online Etymology Dictionary* (Douglas Harper, 2013), www.etymonline.com. Accessed 11 June 2013.

Notes for Entries 47 & 48

Elizabeth Garcia, "God as Intern," *Fire in the Pasture* 184–85. Originally published in *Irreantum* 12.2 (2010): 156–57.

Note for Entry 49

Steven L. Peck, "Winter Gifts," *Fire in the Pasture* 339. Originally published in *Victorian Violet Press Poetry Journal* 5 (2010).

Note for Entries 50 & 51

Paul Swenson, "Negative Space," *Dialogue: A Journal of Mormon Thought* 28.1 (1995): 207. Also *Iced at the Ward, Burned at the Stake* (Salt Lake City: Signature Books, 2003) 44.

Laura Nielson Baxter, "Take Care of Your Soul—It's Flapping in the Breeze," *Fire in the Pasture* 29.

Elisa Pulido, "Dog Walking at Night in a New Neighborhood," *Fire in the Pasture* 363–64. Originally published in *Zocalo Public Square* (19 Apr. 2010).

Is There Deep Play in Heaven?

Epigraph from Paul's poem "Family Plot," *Iced at the Ward, Burned at the Stake* 82.

From "Deseret News' Jerry Johnston" to "ravings of a Scrooge": Jerry Johnston, "Why Waste Space with Ire?," *Deseret Morning News* [Salt Lake City, UT] 20 Dec. 2003, www.deseretnews.com. Accessed 11 June 2013.

From "Stephen Carter suggests" to "stand to lose": Stephen Carter, "Nipples: Exploring Mormonism's 'Negative Space,'" *Sunstone* 138 (Sept. 2005): 69.

From "As Jennifer Reifsneider" to "potential for gain": Jennifer Reifsneider, "Deep Play: Joyful Revelry & Subversive Whimsy in the MAM Collections" (PDF), *Missoula Art Museum* (2007), www.missoulaartmuseum.org. Accessed 11 June 2013.

From "Poetry is a mark" to "muster": Robert Hass, Introduction, *The Best American Poetry 2011* edited by David Lehman and Robert Hass (New York: Scribner, 2001) 18.

From "Stop bleeding" to "I will sink in farther said the knife": May Swenson, "Bleeding," *Iconographs* (New York: Scribner, 1970) 13.

This neighborhood, too, has its underbelly—

From "Woe unto you" to "uncleanness": Matthew 23:27.

"No other success can compensate for failure in the home": James E. McCulloch, *Home: The Savior of Civilization* (Washington, D. C.: Southern Co-Operative League, 1924) 42.

From "the spirit and the body" to "redeemed through Christ's atonement": Doctrine and Covenants 88:15–16.

"The weightier matters of the law": Matthew 23:23.

Note for Entries 52 & 53

Sunni Brown Wilkinson, "Acrobats," *Fire in the Pasture* 476. Originally published in *Weber: The Contemporary West* 25.2 (2009).

Tyler Chadwick, "For the Man in the Red Jacket," *Fire in the Pasture* 105. Originally published in *Mormon Artist* C1 (Nov. 2009): 6.

Laura Hamblin, "To Baptize," *Fire in the Pasture* 201. Originally published in Laura's book, *The Eyes of the Flounder* (Salt Lake City: Signature Books, 2005) 31.

Field Notes on Language and Kinship

26570479R00137

Made in the USA
Lexington, KY
07 October 2013